MEDITERRANEAN
VERNACULAR

MEDITERRANEAN VERNACULAR

A VANISHING ARCHITECTURAL TRADITION ≈ V. I. ATROSHENKO & MILTON GRUNDY

RIZZOLI
NEW YORK

≈

First published in the United States of America in 1991 by

RIZZOLI INTERNATIONAL PUBLICATIONS, INC.

300 Park Avenue South, New York, NY 10010

Copyright © 1991

ANNESS PUBLISHING LIMITED

Library of Congress Cataloging-in-Publication Data

Atroshenko, V. I.

   Mediterranean vernacular: A vanishing architectural

     tradition by Viacheslav

   I. Atroshenko and Milton Grundy: contributing

     editor, Neil Parkyn. p. cm.

   Includes bibliographical references and index.

   ISBN 0-8478-1386-X

   1. Vernacular architecture – Mediterranean Region.

   I. Grundy, Milton. II. Parkyn, Neil, 1943– III. Title

   NA1458.A87 1991

   720′.9182′2–dc20   91-2258 CIP

THE PHOTOGRAPHS

*The vast majority of the photographs in this book are the
work of the author, V. I. Atroshenko. His work alone
appears between pages 1 and 137. Thereafter additional
material is included from other sources to supplement
Mr. Atroshenko's illustrations: these are fully identified
and credited in the Acknowledgements on page 192.
The publishers wish particularly to thank Mr. Robert
O'Dea for permission to include his photographs between
pages 138 and 191.*

CONTENTS

PREFACE

The purpose of this book is to draw attention to a remarkable tradition of vernacular architecture in the Mediterranean basin. The whitewashed village is Near Eastern in origin and has lasted for a thousand years: now mass tourism is threatening its survival. Thirty years ago, Bernard Rudofsky in his exhibition at the Museum of Modern Art in New York, and in his book *Architecture Without Architects*, foresaw the destruction coming through the greed of property speculators. He was right. Much has been lost forever, but enough remains to inspire future architects and town planners, and to revitalize our lives and our communities.

≈ This buttressed facade (OPPOSITE) stands at the edge of the village of Chaouen, in Morocco. Whether it was originally strengthened in the way, or the buttressing is a later addition to allow an extra storey is impossible to say. It is entirely characteristic of the way that vernacular buildings develop organically. Tradition, and the unifying white, soon integrate new features as though they have always been there. There are no 'periods' as in pedigree architecture, and there would, in any case, be no terminology to describe them. ABOVE: detail of a Spanish street.

The photographs we have taken for this book show the genius of long-forgotten builders. Much has still to be done to persuade local governments to preserve their heritage. What we see in these photographs is a communal art — a continuing and spontaneous activity of a whole people. What is quite breathtaking about the vernacular architecture is not so much its antiquity as its originality and invention. The builders shared a common heritage and enjoyed a shared experience. They had the great talent to fit their buildings and villages into the natural surroundings. They did not try to conquer or crush nature. They welcomed the challenge of topography. They carefully defined the community's borders and wisely curbed undesirable expansion. Big is bad, these villages tell us. They are finite as a painting or a piece of music.

For centuries, the inhabitants of these villages lived almost at subsistence level. There is a noticeable absence of unnecessary ornamentation on the buildings. Nothing is 'fashionable'

"In orthodox architectural history, the emphasis is on the work of the individual architect; here the accent is on communal enterprise."

BERNARD RUDOFSKY

≈

or disposable. There is no conspicuous waste. Each village keeps its integrity; it does not lose its soul. There are constant, delightful juxtapositions of strong, natural forms and ever new and varied spaces. Based on the regenerative realities of the locale, this approach to building enabled tradition to act as an invisible hand, guiding the parts towards a unified and ordered completeness. Additions 'grew' adjacent to existing structures. The builders created practical, complex and visually stunning environments without destroying the unity of the village: viewed from afar, it is an elegant, sculptural form that fits naturally into the landscape.

It has practical aspects also: the whitewash protects against disease and reflects the summer heat off the walls; the hillside site provides drainage; the civic identity and co-operation necessary for the preservation and protection of the village has remained intact down the centuries. The whitewashed village is a functional organism that meets the requirements for shelter, work, quiet and social intercourse. Each element feels unique, especially the dwellings, whose scale, asymmetry and flexibility create endless combinations. These villages allow variations of the whole in order to fit individual needs. Here in these beautiful environments we see solutions to many universal problems facing the world, and they are worth emulating.

Today, we appear to have forgotten the art of living in peace and security. We now almost expect chaos, fear, sprawl and ugliness as our preordained fate. The villages in this book display their profound humane qualities with remarkable humility. Since they build and change their own environment carefully over many generations, the villagers never seem to tire of it, and, as they have told us on numerous occasions, they are proud of their achievement. They are proud too of their Arab heritage: at least one white village in Spain has plaques praising their Moorish forebears, and in Amalfi, as we were photographing, a passing villager suggested we go round the corner because 'it is more Saracenic there'.

≈ OPPOSITE: the regions examined in this volume – in order of treatment, Spain (Andelusia and Ibiza); Morocco; Tunisia; Italy and Greece. More detailed maps appear in each section to locate the particular villages and towns that are discussed.

LEFT: an impromptu meeting area in Mykonos exhibits many of the simple virtues of vernacular architecture in the context of a responsible community. There is no formal identification of this area as a public place – it has grown out of a space left where streets cross, and perhaps out of the reluctance of an earlier generation to tear out the trees. Yet, it is immaculately maintained. The background is created with the all-pervading whitewash, and, set against it, the inventiveness of detail is remarkable – typical of the community's care for its environment. Decorative features are picked out in the traditional colours of red and blue, and further ornament is provided by window boxes and pot plants displayed by individual households. Along the skyline chimneys and spires of varying designs comprise a delightfully unostentatious architectural embellishment.

We have travelled widely in the Mediterranean over the past thirty years, photographing these extraordinary villages in Morocco, Tunisia, southern Spain, southern Italy and the Cycladic Islands of Greece. The architectural establishment has in the past dismissed vernacular architecture. We could similarly recall that the musical establishment dismissed the piano works of Schubert until Schnabel began, as late as the 1930s, to include these sublime works in his repertoire. The time has arrived to take a fresh view of vernacular architecture,

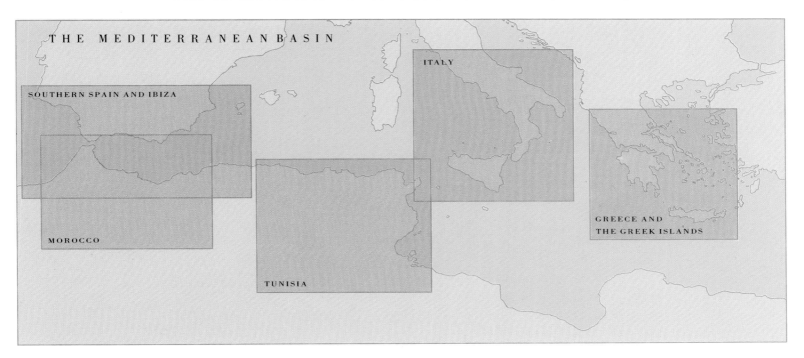

THE MEDITERRANEAN BASIN

SOUTHERN SPAIN AND IBIZA

ITALY

MOROCCO

GREECE AND
THE GREEK ISLANDS

TUNISIA

and to appreciate the qualities in it which appear to elude today's architects, however sophisticated and original.

It is hardly necessary to add our voice to the general abhorrence of many for the desecration of the Mediterranean, especially the Spanish coastline. Unfortunately, the tide of tourist 'development' has overwhelmed what were formerly some of the most attractive of the whitewashed villages, but, happily, examples remain further inland. (Frigiliana, in southern Spain, is one outstanding example of a village that has not been stripped of its pristine charm and identity.)

Whitewashed villages are fragile structures, destroyed almost as easily by well-meaning restoration as by profit-seeking development. The climate of opinion is more 'green' than it was, and to that extent the preservation of these villages may be more likely now than it was in the immediate past. But what is needed is a sense – both locally and internationally – of the importance of what requires to be preserved.

Our approach to this book has been simple and straight-forward: we want the reader to see this white architecture for the beautiful thing it is. Anyone casually turning over the pages which follow may be excused for not knowing whether he is in Italy or Morocco, Greece or Spain. It is apparent that these examples of vernacular architecture belong to the same family. The point is made visually; we do not need to labour it. For this reason the first section of the book – The White Villages – consists of a primarily visual and descriptive tour of the countries of the Mediterranean basin, which provides for the first time a comprehensive comparative documentation of

≈ OPPOSITE: although close to the Mediterranean coast, and subject to a degree of new development, Frigiliana is a fine example of an old village which, although not spectacular in terms of a town such as Casares, has nevertheless retained its atmosphere, style and integrity during the period of its expansion. One has only to compare it to speculative 'Andalusian' tourist village developments along the nearby coastline to appreciate the discrimination and taste which has guided Frigiliana's growth.
LEFT: the architecture of the poor has no history, but nevertheless can be remarkable. These farm buildings are on Djerba, an island off the coast of Tunisia. Although the shores of the island have been developed for tourism, the interior remains traditionally agricultural. The domed and barrel-vaulted construction typifies both the domestic and agricultural buildings of the area. And, as elsewhere, the continuing use of age-old architectural technology means that the vernacular tradition is manifested in both ancient and modern structures.

the vernacular architecture of the region. The second section –
The Influence of the Vernacular – goes on to take a more tech-
nical and analytical view of the village architecture, principally looking towards the future, and examining the irony that,
even as the buildings themselves disappear, their continuing
importance may be assured by their influence on modern
architects and architecture.

Any history of architecture will tell you about famous architects, public buildings and the houses of the rich and powerful. But the poor have no history, their dwellings are rarely
documented, and the people who built them are soon forgotten.
We hope that by writing this book, and by visually recording
these villages, we may have made a small contribution towards
a wider recognition of their importance.

V.I. ATROSHENKO AND MILTON GRUNDY

THE WHITE VILLAGES

≈

" There is much to learn from architecture before it became an expert's art. "
BERNARD RUDOFSKY

INTRODUCTION

Islamic warriors from North Africa – the Moors – entered the Iberian Peninsula in the early part of the eighth century and within forty years had conquered the various small kingdoms into which the area was divided, all except for the most northerly part. It was from the far north that the Christian reconquest began, which ended in the final expulsion of the Moors after an occupation of seven hundred years.

What distinguished the Moors was not their race but their religion. Very few of them were Arabs in the sense that they could trace their ancestry to inhabitants of the Arabian Peninsula, but Arabic was their language and their culture. That culture was in part assimilated from the Byzantine and Persian Empires, much of which had been conquered by the Arabs. Out of that cultural amalgam the Moors developed the white village, generally on a hill-top site or other defensive position. We now find these white villages in Mediterranean Europe and North Africa. The hill-top or hillside site preserved agricultural land and offered defensive advantages. With the return of Christian power, the mosque was demolished to make way for a church, but the format was otherwise retained, villages being enlarged and new ones established on the same pattern.

It was characteristic of the Moorish town that it developed without any overall design. The unplanned streets were narrow and irregular and the houses were entered via a courtyard, which principally served to keep the women from public view. The feature was widely – though not universally – retained after the conquest. It

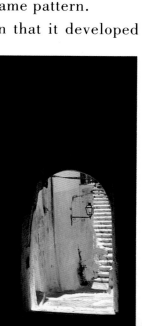

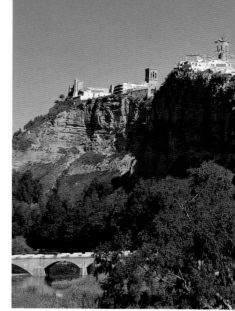

may contain a well, or sometimes a fountain. There are always some trees or plants. And the space serves as a kitchen, a workspace, a laundry, a playing area for children and a place for the family to sit in the evening. The love of plants spreads beyond the inner courtyard: they overflow with abundance from tiny patios and from containers of all sorts on windowsills or steps, or even hung on the wall.

The visitor to one of the whitewashed villages will typically see these pristine dwellings first from a distance, as he rounds a corner or comes over the top of a hill. The sculptural quality of the entire ensemble is immediately apparent. From far away it impinges upon the eye not as a collection of discrete buildings but as a form which emerges from, but is nevertheless closely related to, the landscape on which it rests. The effect is aesthetically compelling. It may be explained in terms of building technology, skills and materials; in terms of shelter, deflection of sunlight, protection from wind and overall adaptation to environment and climate; or in terms of the long tradition which unified the whole while not denying the nuances of individualism.

≈ LEFT: a traditional, high, narrow street, in Arcos de la Frontera, with an arch supporting the buildings on either side. As the pathway splits at the end, the fork and chamfered cornering is embellished with a simple column infill. The height of the buildings provides deep shade. Climate, as so often inspires every architectural decision. ABOVE: the precipitous cliff-top location of Arcos de la Frontera.

The overall whiteness is incandescent. It is achieved by endless whitewashing. For the Japanese, physical cleanliness is a correlative of spiritual purity; in Mediterranean towns and villages, whitewashing certainly has practical uses – making streets more negotiable after dark, maintaining a level of hygiene, discouraging flies, repelling heat – but it is done with such assiduity that, here too, it appears to have an overwhelmingly aesthetic or symbolic importance to the inhabitants. Innumerable layers, of which the latest is quite recent, cover whatever imperfections lie beneath. Walls, roofs, doorsteps, stairs, even some parts of the street are unified in the prevailing white.

≈ ABOVE: Vernacular architectural forms permeate the smallest corners: in this Ibizan backyard the tiny outhouse is domed in the Moorish style and the effect is completed by terracotta pots.

As we move into and through the village, we are aware of a rich and complicated environment. First impressions may be primarily aesthetic. There is a simplicity and lack of orna-mentation. The houses, while conforming to a common type, vary subtly one from another; there is a profusion of stunning detail – the chamfered corners, the mysterious vistas, the changing levels, the glimpsed courtyards, and so on. The pervasive whiteness blankets these villages with distinctive uniformity, and signifies a well cared-for public space – far removed from the public spaces of most human communities, of which Tokyo or New York may stand for the worst. The point is not the whiteness but the degree of attention given to main-taining these public spaces, and the neglected urban habita-tions of today are doubly stark and disturbing when compared to the whitewashed villages of the Mediterranean.

Beyond the merely aesthetic impression, we become aware of the quality of the environment as a whole. The motor car and the delivery van have only limited access and, in consequence, there is much carrying and cart-pushing. And because of the

≈ **17**

≈ ABOVE: a Christian church rests on top of a hill in Ibiza, where in previous centuries a mosque might well have been situated. The whitewashing tradition extends to religious buildings, as well as domestic dwellings, throughout the Mediterranean basin.

restricted narrowness of the inner roads there is not only a degree of quietness and freedom from atmospheric pollution but also endless opportunities for the sort of social intercourse which we are nowadays trying to recapture in our 'pedestrianized' areas.

There was never any overall plan for the development of these villages. The compositions and the vistas we see are the result of piecemeal development and organic growth in accordance with a shared tradition. This is especially apparent in the construction of the stairways — both the private staircases by which an upper storey is reached directly from the street, and the various level-changes of the thoroughfares themselves. Unlike the standardized and mechanical designs prescribed by our building regulations, stairs here have rhythm and pauses, landings and ramps, and variety in depth, width and height. This is folk art as truly as are the ballad and folk song. It is something we have lost entirely, and it is hard for us to imagine how the picturesque juxtapositions of solid and void, the surprising views, the elegantly placed arches or windows, could have derived from a shared aesthetic without the necessity for planning or other controls.

It is true that life at or close to subsistence level enforces an economy which manifests itself in a lack of ornamentation, the utilization of living rock, and a general simplicity — not to say austerity — in the size and shape of dwelling houses. And it is true that an intense conservatism may enforce the use of the whitewashed cube, and that hillside gradient sites necessitated streets more or less parallel to the contour line. But economic and geographic constraints do not explain the aesthetic triumph of the result. It is simplistic to see the custom to which the builders of these highly sympathetic complexes adhered as a

≈ LEFT: the human scale of the vernacular settlement is exemplified by this typical whitewashed church on Mykonos. Other than its dome and restrained spire, the building barely rises above the domestic houses that surround and abut it. The play of light and shadow in these streets is extraordinary. Changing from hour to hour with the movement of the sun, each space presents a dozen different moods during the course of a single day. Visitors from heavily urban cultures – increasingly immune to the possibilities of being delighted by (or even interested in) the built environment – can be surprised by the inspiration such simple scenes provide. BELOW LEFT: The belfry of St Jorge, Ibiza.

simple prohibition of change; it contained a life and vitality to which we can ourselves respond – especially, perhaps, because of our sense of the loss of such a tradition in the societies which we now inhabit.

It is telling that in these villages the general welfare of the inhabitants is not subordinated to the pursuit of profit and 'progress'. Seemingly, they have learnt to live and let live. They know how to keep peace with their neighbours. They have not been reduced to automobile appendages. The qualities we find in these villages include light, ventilation, warmth in winter, freshness in summer, and privacy. There are garbage cans but one does not see them littering the alleys and streets. The proud housewife keeps her 'patch' clean and healthy for the community's general welfare. Interior patios are flower-adorned family spaces of charm and tranquility.

It is plain that this environment bears no evidence of the drawing board: it has the feeling of an organism and not of a machine, of an unselfconscious adaptation to a succession of needs and opportunities within a unifying tradition. The whitewashed village has a human scale to which we are not accustomed. It has grown slowly and organically; the place appears to be made up of virtually identical cubes (though we shall see on closer examination that there is a surprising variation of detail), yet the overall effect is the very opposite of dull or repetitious. Just what factors have come together to produce so magical a sight we may find it difficult to analyze, yet we are drawn to explore it further.

≈ **19**

≈ An essential
ingredient of the
vernacular 'mix' is the
informal public space – an
architectural element that
modern planners are
struggling to recreate in the
mainly unsuccessful
'pedestrian precincts' of
new towns around the
world. In these villages
traditional meeting-places
are not grand, well-planned
squares or piazzas, but
areas formed haphazardly
where the contour broadens
the road or where two
streets cross each other.
This well-maintained space
in Frigiliana becomes a
restaurant in the summer
months. Although public,
in the sense that it is
shared by all, these areas
are commonly kept clean
and decorated by the
people whose houses
surround them: the hanging
baskets and potted plants
to the right characterize the
individual's pride in the
community and the face it
presents to the world.

≈ OPPOSITE: a feature of the vernacular style is the 'unclaimed' space – neither fully public nor fully private – which occurs naturally where streets meander to an end or where an alley leads off to service a small group of dwellings. In more urban communities such spaces would be staked out and fenced off, but the relaxed nature of these settlements, and the willingness to share, means that territorialism is a rarity. Again, although the space is not 'owned', someone has taken on the responsibility to ornament it with that most evocative of Mediterranean garnishes – the geranium in a whitewashed oil-can.

RIGHT: even in an impoverished country such as Morocco the streets are kept immaculately clean and tidy by the inhabitants. The owners of these houses cannot afford to re-render the facades of their dwellings, but the floors are uncluttered by litter and a little light blue colouring – traditional to the region – is added here and there.

●

SOUTHERN SPAIN AND IBIZA

Most of the photographs in this section are of scenes in Andalusia. This is a large region, comprising Spain's eight southern provinces – Huelva, Seville, Cádiz, Córdoba, Málaga, Jaén, Granada, and Almería – extending from the Portuguese frontier in the west to the border of Murcia in the east, and including the whole of the southern coast of Spain. This coast, with its agreeable winter climate and many beaches, has been 'developed' for tourism in a manner which makes Florida seem tasteful, but the world of package tours and urbanization is only a thin strip along the coast: a few miles inland there is a charming and unspoiled country-side dotted with agricultural buildings and containing many white villages.

Moslems from North Africa landed in Spain in 711 AD and in a short time came to rule the entire peninsula. This was immediately followed by a Christian war of 'reconquest', but it was not until the end of the fifteenth century that Granada, the last Moslem bastion in Spain, fell to the Christian forces. In light of the Arab expansion across North Africa which brought

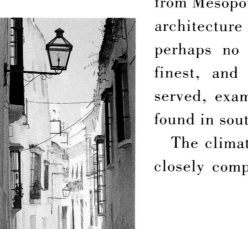

from Mesopotamia the kind of vernacular architecture illustrated in this book, it is perhaps no surprise that some of the finest, and incidentally the best preserved, examples of this style are to be found in southern Spain today.

The climatic imperatives in Spain are closely comparable to those endured in

≈ OPPOSITE: the well-favoured settlement of Almunecar built its defences principally against maritime attack. In a siege, the inhabitants could swiftly move up into the virtually unassailable fortress, which had a water supply and had developed storage facilities for the village's grain stocks with that eventuality in mind. Its dual source of income – fishing and crops – is reflected in the comfortable cleanliness and well-kempt whiteness of the buildings. The essentially feudal social origins of the vernacular are emphasized by the contrast between the individuality of scale and architecture of the fort and the sameness of all the other buildings. Even with differentials in wealth, no other inhabitant ever saw fit to erect a dwelling of a differing size or design that copied or challenged the imposing central structure. LEFT: an atmospheric street scene from Arcos de la Frontera.

≈ In Casares, the long, white buildings that sit at the peak of the hill to the right of the tower are, in fact, a cemetery. Land is too scarce on the hill-top to allow space for a normal graveyard, and it must have been thought too dangerous or clumsy to manhandle coffins down the steep and narrow streets to a burial site at a lower level. The inhabitants solved the problem by placing the bodies above the ground in layers of individual, barrel-vaulted crypts which, joined together and whitewashed, now rise up to five or six storeys high and can be seen from miles around. Surely nowhere else in the world are the dead allowed such a spectacular and memorable position in their society.

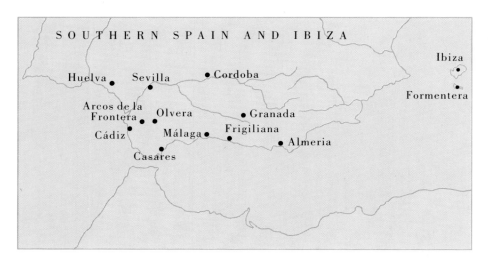

SOUTHERN SPAIN AND IBIZA

Huelva · Sevilla · Cordoba · Ibiza

Formentera

Arcos de la Frontera · Olvera · Granada

Cádiz · Málaga · Frigiliana · Almeria

Casares

≈ BELOW: in Frigiliana the Moorish heritage is evident in the pavement design and architectural detailing, but is most obviously emphasized by the plaque on the wall commemorating the suffering of the Moorish inhabitants who were brutally victimized after an uprising in 1569. This area of the old town has been changed and modified over the years, but still retains the essential characteristics of its Moorish ancestry: the irregularity and disparity of surfaces; the changing street levels; the narrow spaces between the dwellings; and the delightful air of mystery created by the shifting perspective, the hidden corners and the half-seen alleys.

parts of Arabia – the intense solar radiation during the long day, the cool nights, the strong wind blowing sand and dust, the high humidity in coastal areas. In addition the requirement that a dwelling should be so planned as to provide privacy for the family, and in particular the womenfolk was also of prime importance in both locations. It is natural, therefore, that the basic form of the typical dwelling – massive, inward-looking and attuned to the demanding climate – should have remained unchanged in the 'export' model.

It is not always recalled that Moslem civilization in Spain represented a beacon of learning and culture in a Europe which was barely emerging from the Dark Ages. Sophisticated, elegant monuments of this civilization remain to be seen today, such as the former mosque in Cordoba, and Alhambra in Granada. In general, the Spaniards still seem to regard the centuries of their Moslem history as a kind of cultural penetration in which they can take some pride. This is due, in part, to the very high quality and distinction of many of the artifacts the Moors left behind as a legacy, especially when compared to the rather heavy-handed 'colonial' buildings of the Turkish regime in Greece, which was a much more oppressive occupation. In Frigiliana, for example, tablets on the walls recall, sympathetically, the sufferings of the last Moslem inhabitants of the village.

≈ OPPOSITE: from a distance, the typical Spanish whitewashed village appears dense and compact, not arising out of the landscape so much as settling over it like an organism, as the shape of the village so closely reflects the underlying contours of the land. This effect is finely described – in particular reference to this village, Olvera – by Norman Carver in his *Iberian Villages* (see bibliography): 'It is a geometry at once integrated with and distinct from the landscape which sustains it – a form determined as much by nature as by man and his institutions.'

The village, dominated by its wonderful Christian basilica and Moorish keep, seems to float across the landscape like a cloud, shimmering in the heat like a mirage. The defensive hill-top location was plainly important, and now gives a pleasing finiteness – so different from the suburban and light-industrial sprawl of other communities – as the settlement is prevented from spreading downwards across the rich agricultural land that supports it. It can never become the 'historic centre' or 'old town' within a newer, larger megapolis.

Olvera has around 12,500 inhabitants, and is a centre of religion and pilgrimage.

The best known of the villages illustrated in this section is Arcos de la Frontera. It is built on a dramatic rocky spike, with a river at its foot. It is perhaps more properly described as a small town, with a population of nearly 26,000 people. It has a fine main square, with an early Renaissance church, and a spectacular view from one side.

Ibiza, one of the Balearic Islands of Spain, enjoys a more temperate climate than Andalusia, but it too had its period of Moorish rule and here too the vernacular building is white. White architecture is to be found in the older parts of the main towns and manifests itself with most distinction in the churches, many of which are illustrated here.

≈ The unified colouring of the buildings, and their similarity in size and shape, mean that the eye is not drawn to particular architectural features but takes in the vernacular village as a single entity – the exception being the church, mosque or castle, which generally dominates the scene. Even quite ordinary churches are exaggerated into magnificence by the contrast in scale, texture and colouring with the unity and simplicity of the domestic dwellings. This town, Arcos de la Frontera, is in the south of the Iberian Peninsula, in Cadiz, close to the border with Malaga, due north of the Strait of Gibraltar. The view shows the protection afforded to the town by the sheer cliffs dropping down to the Guadalete river. It was an early stronghold of the Moors, from which further incursions were launched, until it was ceded to Spanish warlords as a reward for their part in the *Reconquista*. The town still maintains an aura of mystery – folklore associates it with witchcraft and low magic.

≈ The middle-distance views on these pages – both of Setenil (BOTTOM LEFT and MIDDLE RIGHT) and of Frigiliana – show how the overall impression of a townscape begins to break down as one approaches, from a unified white mass into its component cubic building blocks and sloping tiled roofs. The effect of contour becomes more evident, delineated by streets clinging to the narrow terraces cut into the hillside.

The town of Setenil is about twelve miles north of Ronda, in the ravine of the Guadalporcun river. It is very ancient, and in several areas of the town there are still the remains of troglodytic dwellings – often with modern housing now built out of or on to old cliff apertures. Much of it has been built in quite recent times, and, like Frigiliana, it is an interesting example of a town in which the vernacular tradition has truly survived, with new joining old almost invisibly in a style that has existed for centuries. Its inland location protects it from mass tourism, meaning that the scale of the new buildings and the materials from which they are fashioned are exactly in keeping with the existing forms – evolving from and responding to the needs of the community, rather than

from external demands or incursions. The contrast between the irregularly disposed buildings at the base of the village – where the land is flatter and allows more personal choice – and the linear arrangement higher up – where the disciplines imposed by contour come into play – are striking. Unusually, the church is not in the centre of the town, nor quite on the brow of the hill: it stands separate, with a few houses clustering around and between it and the decaying fortress.

≈ On entering the vernacular town or village – in this case Frigiliana – the effects of contour on design become immediately evident. The normal concerns of defence and the desire to conserve farmable land led to Frigiliana's hillside location, and its consequent development on a multitude of different levels. The answer to the access problems confronted by builders in a townscape which works on so many levels is the stepped street – a solution which adds a great deal of character to these settlements and affords many opportunities for decoration.

≈ RIGHT: a street in Frigiliana showing that the builders were prepared to work against the contour, as well as along it – though the steepness here must have caused considerable problems in construction. Just as the modern urban dweller who purchases a second property in a rural community is liable to condemn his indigenous neighbour for leaving dirty farming equipment on view in the yard, the architect-traveller or critic can find himself baulking at the sight of 'ugly' junction boxes and casually draped electrical wiring. But 'vernacular' is a description of the way that ordinary people live – not a celebration of the picturesque, or of the noble savage. The real message in a scene such as this comes in the sense of unavoidable community that it engenders: the proximity of the dwellings; the well-ordered congestion; and the semi-public, semi-private spaces that interrupt the stepping of the street. LEFT: a slightly different, but equally charming, effect is created by the same elements in Arcos de la Frontera.

≈ LEFT: the facade to the left of the courtyard is recent, and obviously lacks the characteristic charm of the ancient rock on the right, with its irregular surface and interesting texture. Yet its details are all 'authentic' in the vernacular tradition: the courtyard area is shade-bearing; the new facade is properly and newly whitewashed; the ironwork is in keeping with the window-dressing of the region, and the street surface is decorated and maintained in the village style. ABOVE: again, new meets old in perfect harmony.

≈ Vernacular architecture in Ibiza stands mid-way –
both geographically and figuratively – between the rougher
and more primitive forms of North Africa, and the slightly
more formalized and organized systems of the other
European countries discussed. Its climate is the most
equable in the Balearic Islands, although fresh water is in
limited supply being dependent on rainfall or ground water
sourced from deep wells.

After early visits from the Greeks, Phoenicians,
Carthaginians and Romans, the most significant influence
on Ibizan culture was, as elsewhere in southern Spain,
Arabic. The Moors first took the island, which they called
Yebisah, in 711, but, after several periods of conquest and
expulsion (they were most notably driven away by
Charlemagne in 798) it was not until the early tenth
century that they established a lasting foothold. The Moors
were finally forced off of the island in 1235, when an army
under the command of the Archbishop of Tarragona retook
Ibiza for Jaime I. It was immediately re-Christianized, and
it was at this time that the Moorish mosques would have
been torn down or converted into churches – the buildings,
however, retained a heavily Moorish flavour, and new

architecture was also naturally influenced by the Arabic style which had been in fashion on the island, periodically, for nearly five hundred years. This church (LEFT and BELOW LEFT) in San Jorge, a few miles south-west of Ibiza town, and three-quarters of a mile inland, dates from the fourteenth century, and is fortified – the island remained continually under threat from raids by Moorish and Turkish pirates based in North Africa. Although the Moors had left Ibiza a hundred years before its construction, the church still shows their influence and is very similar to mosques in Tunisia in its use of solid blocks only occasionally pierced by doors and small window apertures. The hand-made surface identifies it as a member of the vernacular family.

The church of Santa Eulalia (BELOW RIGHT) stands at the top of the hill that dominates Santa Eulalia del Rio, Ibiza's third largest town. It was built in the fourteenth century on the ruins of an Arab mosque. Ibiza was an important part of the Mediterranean trade network. This encouraged cultural as well as commercial interchange, and the church was further refined and developed in the sixteenth century by the Italian architect Calvi. ABOVE RIGHT: a detail of an arch from the church of San Carlos.

≈ This group of images once again shows that the vernacular tradition is not restricted to secular or ecclesiastical structures, but crosses into every type of building. The churches of Santa Eulalia (BOTTOM LEFT) and San Carlos (TOP LEFT) share a style with a simple house (TOP RIGHT) just outside Ibiza town, and a small courtyard in the village of San Carlos, which contains an oven built to a pattern of great antiquity (BOTTOM RIGHT). The manner of vernacular building is unchanging — whatever its purpose. We are accustomed to ovens requiring a shift in design or at least different materials, but this one is simply integrated into the adjacent walling and the dwelling it serves. The eighteenth-century church in San Carlos uses the vernacular style playfully. The facade extends to the right of the bell-tower, but the building itself does not extend behind it, and the chamfered corners and buttressing appear to have no purpose or function other than decoration.

MOROCCO

Moorish forces, bringing Islam from Arabia, reached Morocco in the late seventh century. By the eighth century the country was fully Islamized and has remained so to this day. It was never Turkish, but retained its independence through various dynasties and had periods of great prosperity, echoed by artistic and intellectual growth. It underwent a century of French domination from the 1840s, and more recently the Spaniards have occupied parts of the north, but otherwise Morocco has always been autonomous and has enjoyed a long continuity of cultural and religious traditions. It is perhaps for this reason that these examples of white architecture in Morocco come from settlements which are not mere villages: Chaouen is a small town, but Tetouan could properly be called a city.

Chaouen is a hill town which was founded by Moslems fleeing the Christian reconquest of Andalusia in the fifteenth century. For this very obvious reason and because of the parallels in climate, it is not surprising that the refugees returned to familiar models when building their new homes. Its situation makes it a natural fortress: it is blessed with many springs, which have obvious advantages in times of siege as well as serving the more peaceful purpose of nourishing its luxuriant gardens. Tetouan, built on the ruins of a first-century settlement, was founded in the fifteenth century, when it, too, received refugees from Andalusia.

It is necessary to bear in mind, when viewing these buildings, that Morocco is considerably less wealthy than even Spain, and as a consequence the scenes tend to have a rougher appearance. Walls and road surfaces are less well maintained than in Spain, but the townscape here is undoubtedly of the

≈ This scene from Tetouan, particularly the detail of the ceramic tiles on the steps is reminiscent of Spain. This is not surprising considering the antecedents of a town still sometimes known locally as 'the daughter of Granada'. The settlement has a long history, dating back to the Berber city of Tamuda, which was destroyed by the Romans in the first century AD; but 'modern' Tetouan was founded in the fifteenth century by Muslim and Jewish refugees from Spain and Portugal. Links remained strong between Spain and Tetouan until the twentieth century. During this period the town was the capital of Spain's Moroccan territories. This charming covered street, although in need of some pavement repair, is otherwise well-maintained.

same family, and it is logical to deduce that, whatever influences from Islamic Spain may be represented in the grand houses and palaces, the fifteenth-century refugees found and further developed in Morocco just the kind of vernacular building they had left behind.

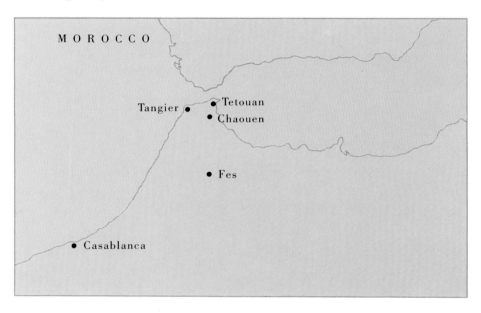

≈ The Moors first invaded Morocco in the seventh century, on a holy mission to spread the word of Islam. They called the region *el Maghreb el Aqsa* ('farthest to the West') and, having eventually won over the Berbers to Islam, indelibly implanted their culture and architectural styling, as can be seen (OPPOSITE) in this narrow, decorated street in Tetouan. The fascinating township of Chaouen (BELOW LEFT) sits high in the Rif mountains.

Today, Tetouan is an unattractive modern city with a small area of vernacular building remaining. Chaouen, in contrast, has retained much of its historical character. An Islamic holy city, it opened to non-Moslems only recently and because of its religious status has been virtually untouched by modern development. Chaouen remains encapsulated in the past.

≈ The arches serve as buttresses to the walls on either side of this street in Tetouan. This is a feature which frequently recurs elsewhere: variations on this form are to be found in southern Spain, southern Italy, and further north in Venice and Provence. The herring-bone gully provides drainage – hygiene was necessarily a high priority in early urban developments. The importance of hygiene is further evident in the ubiquitous use of whitewash, which as well as acting as a primitive disinfectant, carries light into these alleyways.

≈ The township of Chaouen (the name means 'see the
peaks') sits on the edge of the Rif mountains, forty miles
from Tetouan. Until recently a holy place to which non-
Moslems were not admitted, and offering, in any case, no
obvious attractions to mass-tourism, Chaouen has escaped
the ravages of commercial and industrial development.
Indeed, so isolated was it that when the Spanish took it in
1926 as the last act in extinguishing the rising by the
Berber leader, Abd el Krim, they found the inhabitants
employing craft skills in their everyday businesses which
had totally disappeared in the outside world over four
hundred years before. Chaouen accommodated many
immigrants retreating from the Christian conquest of
southern Spain in the fifteenth century.

≈ On this and the following pages is depicted the *medina* at Chaouen – this being the term in the Arab world for the old, or original town. This is a fascinating area, originally split into distinct quarters – Berber, Jewish, Moroccan, and Andalusian. The Jewish and Andalusian 'ghettos' may be explained by the desire of the refugees to stick together for security and to reproduce, to some degree, the lifestyle they had left behind them in Spain. These two streets are in the Andalusian quarter: iron-work over the windows is prevalent here, and there is a tradition in this section to pick out the tips of the roof tiles in white. The woman is caught in the act of smothering herself in a traditional white over-robe.

≈ The Mediterranean vernacular style, while displaying common features in all the countries in which it has been adopted, has nevertheless adapted itself to varying cultural and social requirements. Here, for example, in a Moslem country, the desire for domestic privacy and the concern of the men to isolate the women of the family results in very few windows opening onto the street at ground floor level.

≈ The neglected and broken road reflects Chaouen's poverty and lack of sophistication. The inhabitants have neither the money nor the inclination to extend or modernize their homes with the glazed doors and tiled steps that are increasingly beginning to adorn and disfigure vernacular dwellings in other regions. A closer examination reveals that, although money may not be available for improvements, or even basic structural maintenance, what *is* there is well swept and whitewashed. In addition, the local custom of spreading the traditional blue colouring onto the walls creates a delightful, cool, tranquil effect.

≈ In steeply sloping streets the drainage channels form a perfect natural outlet for waste, and, though hardly noticed by the residents, to the visitor they add a distinctive and interesting touch. This particular image seems to sum up the vernacular charm of the region. The diverse and intriguing sculptural shapes and their disposition upwards from the foreground to the middle-distance gives distinction to a simple passageway. Nothing is uniform but all is in harmony: the invisible hand of tradition links the public and private spaces in a way that has no parallel in urban communities. A gifted set-designer would be hard tested to achieve such an effortless result.

≈ The whitewashed rubble surface (ABOVE), which gives such interesting patterns of light and shade under the Mediterranean sunlight, is conspicuous here. The use of blue (RIGHT) for the woodwork of doors and windows occurs elsewhere – notably in Greece. Traditionally, it protected the openings in the house against penetration by evil spirits. Only in Morocco, however, does the blue spread over the walls, often in very pale shades, and the locals claim that, in addition to its other properties, it keeps the mosquitos away. More striking than in even the poorest areas of Italy and Greece, the streets here have a hand-made quality. The rise of the steps is irregular and the levelling of them is erratic, with living rock, or perhaps stones from earlier buildings, incorporated into the fabric of the structures.

≈ The network of alleyways of the Chaouen *medina* would cause nervousness and apprehension if it were put down in one of our urban capitals. It offers so many hiding places and opportunities to be surprised. But here, in the tranquillity and security of a small, close-knit community, one can safely rediscover the pleasure of architectural mystery and intrigue, and enjoy the revelation of whether a half-hidden entry leads into another alley, or into somebody's house or courtyard. Here in the quiet depths of the town, surrounded by white rock and stone, it is easy to be reminded of the origins of the vernacular in primitive cave-dwellings. RIGHT: another hidden corner in the *medina*.

≈59

≈ The *medina* at Tetouan, in which this street lies, is not large, but nevertheless contains over twenty mosques – all of them small and understated on a vernacular, human scale. Although many times the size of Chaouen and much wealthier, the town displays its seniority not by adopting grand or modern styles, but by the merest touches of embellishment to the same building systems. The ceramic decoration, the hint of colour, and the general smartness and higher standard of repair, are the only significant differences.

TUNISIA

Whitewashed buildings are not as prevalent in Tunisia as they are in southern Spain and Morocco. It may be that in former times they were more common, as a rather debased form occurs in the medina at Sousse, and more convincing examples are to be found in parts of the old town in Hammamet. What is now Tunisia was Islamized, along with the rest of North Africa, in the late seventh and early eighth centuries, and it may be logical to suppose that white architecture was once more widespread than these remains imply. Between the fall of the Roman and the rise of the Turkish Empires, the area had a violent history, and it is not surprising that few monuments of earlier times survive intact. The examples described here were found in isolated places: the wonderful *ghorfas* of Ksar Haddada, and, in the desert, far from the coast, the mosque — one of many — in the middle of the Island of Djerba, in the south, close to Libya.

A feature of the buildings at Ksar Haddada is the use of barrel vaulting. The barrel vault is of great antiquity. Examples may be seen in ancient Assyrian friezes in the British Museum and it was of course a feature widely used in the church building of Early Christian and subsequently Romanesque periods. It occurs in the white architecture of various countries (see for example the church in Amorgos, in Greece, page 106). As explained in detail later, it is also a building element favoured by several pioneers of Modern architecture, such as Le Corbusier, Josep Lluis Sert and Louis Kahn. The barrel vault creates a very strong sense of directional enclosure of space and is therefore, quite apart from the ease of its construction, an appropriate method of roofing basic cellular areas.

≈ It is very unusual in vernacular architecture to discover a decorative element integrated into the building's structure (as opposed to an ornamental device attached to it). This striking feature (OPPOSITE) has, unlike the buttresses to either side, no apparent structural purpose, but its shape and the planes of light and shadow it creates, have an abstract exuberance, reminiscent of the sculptural work of Anthony Caro. This mosque is on Djerba, a small island off the Tunisian coast close to the Libyan border. LEFT: palm trees are part of the landscape's architecture in Tunisia.

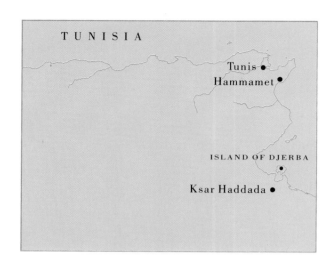

TUNISIA

Tunis ●
Hammamet ●

ISLAND OF DJERBA
●

Ksar Haddada ●

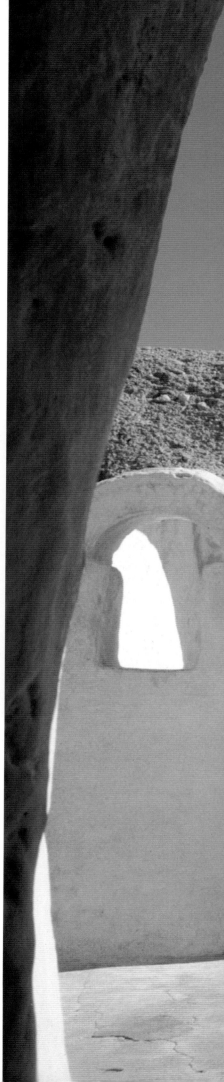

≈ The interior (ABOVE), and exterior (RIGHT), of an ancient Berber grain store at Ksar Haddada. Such a granary is properly called a *ghorfa* – a long oblong room with a barrel-vaulted roof. These buildings would be arranged in four rectangles around a central court, forming a fortified central courtyard-cum-market area called a *ksar* – hence Ksar Haddada. The *ghorfa* and *ksar* are for commercial use only: domestic housing would grow out from and around these centres. The Berbers of Tunisia, like their Moroccan brethren, are a people who prefer independence. Driven into the hills by Moorish invaders, they developed networks of these complex settlements, some of which are still used today. The workings of the *ghorfa* and *ksar* are examined in detail in the following pages, as this was the primary building unit in the Tunisian vernacular tradition.

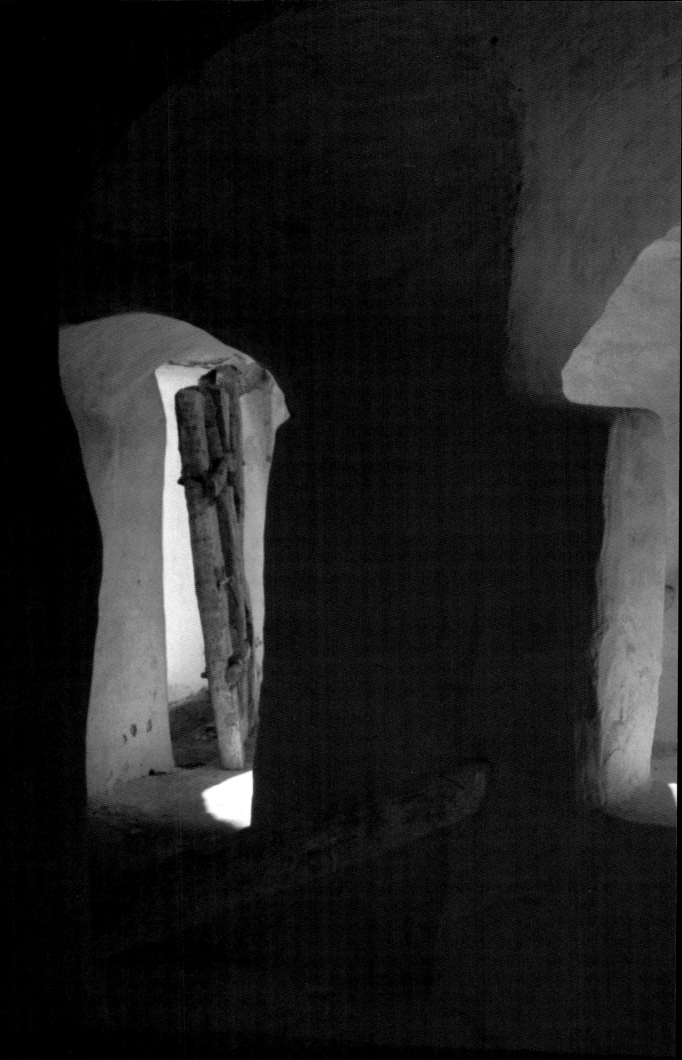

≈ Another *ghorfa* at
Ksar Haddada. This type of
building relies almost
exclusively on cut stone,
rubble and plaster. The
wooden balustrade seen
here is rare, and wood is
hardly ever used in the
construction of the building
frames.

The irregularity of the
use of building materials in
the construction illustrates
the direct involvement of
the builder with the
architectural process.
These buildings were not
designed on a drawing
board and then
scientifically erected with
reference to the architect's
plans. In effect, the
craftsman made up his plan
as he went along – adapting
the shape, materials and
construction method as new
problems arose to be
solved. This personal
architecture – the steps
rising without the aid of the
set-square, and the walls
climbing without the
assistance of the plumb
line – makes a direct
appeal to the sensibilities
that is quite different from
the reaction generated by
more formal architecture,
however elegant or
brilliant.

≈ Single-level *ghorfas* exist, but more often they are built on top of one another, sometimes many storeys high. To haul the grain up to the higher floors a projecting pole was built into the wall: more elaborate modern versions can still be seen on warehouse buildings around the world, notably in Amsterdam, and even on the designer-converted storehouses of London's Covent Garden. Ksar Haddada is many hundreds of years old and no longer inhabited, but it has been carefully restored and redecorated in the traditional colours and style.

≈ The *ksar* – in the specific sense of the interior,
enclosed area formed by the group of four *ghorfas* – was
used in times of peace for trading and as an informal
meeting place, and in times of danger as a first line of
fortified defence. When an attack materialized the settlers
would have been much more likely to withdraw to the local
kalaa (a fort similar to the castles of Spain) where the
defences were stronger and they could collectively defend
the community.

≈ The *ksar* became a pattern of steps, stairs and
walkways. While allowing workers ease of access to
different areas of the store, the elaborate internal
structuring also creates superb aesthetic effects,
especially in the dramatic play of light and shadow – an
example of remarkable form following a quite simple
function. It is interesting to see repeated here, in a quite
different and very flat terrain, many of the characteristic
elements of the hillside vernacular – changing levels,
steps, and a sculptural response to materials in an organic
unity with the landscape.

≈ Again the universality of the vernacular approach is emphasized: it describes both the massive buttresses of the mosque and also the tiny group of barrel-vaulted, dome-roofed wash-houses beyond. This mosque on Djerba is set inland, away from the high-rise hotels and tourist developments of the island's coastline. Djerba is dotted with mosques (some of quite unusual types), churches and synagogues. The island is famous for its religious freedom: it became a sanctuary in times of religious intolerance for those who wished to follow unfashionable or outlawed faiths – particularly Moslems of the Kharijite sect.

≈ Djerba is not the perfect place to farm – the climate is dry, and the soil sandy – but the pace of life is rhythmic, slow and amenable, and the traditional farming methods are well adapted to cope with the conditions. Palms, fruit trees and olive trees are readily cultivated. Ironically this apparently sleepy farmhouse is situated near Houmt Souk, the commercial centre of the island, and the location of the airport. With its round arched entrance door, its barrel-vaulted appendages, and the buttressed cube which forms its body, this farm building differs in hardly any essential from most of the mosques in the region. The entire complex is inward-looking: the few openings are small and randomly placed.

≈ If one did not already know that Le Corbusier was influenced by the Mediterranean vernacular, it would be immediately evident on viewing this mosque near Houmt Souk (ABOVE, TOP, AND LEFT). His masterpiece at Ronchamp, the pilgrimage chapel of Notre Dame du Haut (illustrated on page 181), has similar buttressing, a similar outside staircase, similar use of small windows irregularly positioned within thick walls, and an overall similarity of 'massiveness' and sculptural bulk. Both buildings reflect even earlier models, such as the famous monastery at Amorgos, in the Cyclades Islands of Greece.

≈ RIGHT: the village of
Sperlonga is conscious of
its debt to Moslem culture,
even to the point of
emphasizing the 'Arabic
heritage' in the official
guidebook. The stone
doorway on the left appears
to be a later addition, but it
sits nicely with the earlier,
truly vernacular doorway
on the right. The archways
over the street add an
element of decoration – one
is curved and the other
slightly pointed: such
skyline embellishment has
been noted before, and
similar arches are seen at
Arcos de la Frontera.
Again reminiscent of
Morocco, the door pinned
back against the wall halfway up the street echoes
the doors in the *medina*
which in earlier
generations served to
segregate the different
ethnic quarters at night.

ITALY

Some of the best examples of white architecture are to be found in southern Italy: Sperlonga, a beautifully preserved small town on the coast of north Naples, the villages of Capri and the towns along the Amalfi Coast south of Naples. A related, though somewhat different, style of white building exists in Apulia. At no time did the Naples area come under Moslem (Saracenic rule); Sicily, which did, has few examples. The rarity of whitewashed villages in Sicily is in no doubt the result of many years of poverty and neglect, but their presence further north is unsurprising, for there were many intellectual, commercial and diplomatic contacts between the maritime cities of the mainland and the Saracenic civilizations in Sicily and North Africa.

Sperlonga is wonderfully unspoiled. The town overlooks an

attractive sandy beach, but it is protected by law from indiscriminate building development. Recent building has been almost wholly confined to the plain below, and the hilltown itself retains the characteristics of the typical white village. In the villages of Capri, in Amalfi and in Minori the remains of the white villages must be sought out with some assiduity: layer upon layer of later buildings lie above the arched alleyways of an earlier epoch.

≈ Sperlonga is on the west coast of Italy, about sixty-five miles north-west of Naples and sixty miles south-east of Rome. It is one of the few remaining Italian whitewashed Mediterranean vernacular villages, and it is protected by a special government order restricting building development in the area. As mentioned earlier, it has many Arabic qualities, and this street (OPPOSITE) could have come straight out of the *medina* at Chaouen. This is a particularly 'sculptural' corner of the village, encompassing all the vernacular elements already identified in the Spanish villages: changing levels; steps and stairways; narrow streets clinging to the contours; living rock incorporated into the fabric of the buildings; and the traditional whitewash. More steps in Sperlonga are seen (LEFT) in detail.

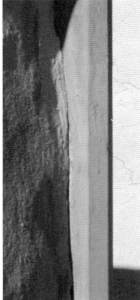

≈ The mosque seen on
the previous page,
glimpsed through the open
entrance in the outer wall.
The door is painted in a
traditional local colour
(seen in detail, ABOVE).

Buildings such as this
are characterized by the
lack of emphasis given to
the units of construction.
Rarely does one see a
pillar, beam, or lintel, and
never a discrete brick or
stone that obviously
indicates the nature of the
fabric. Materials for
vernacular buildings were,
and are, 'found' locally: it
is only in pedigree
architecture, where money
is available and unusual
and expensive materials
can be purchased and
imported, that the
highlighting of the
building's fabric becomes a
stylistic device.

≈ Its beauty and consequent attractions as a holiday centre make Sperlonga a community of mixed wealth: there is still poverty in some of the older areas of the village, but the income from tourists has allowed many inhabitants to improve their habitations. This can be seen here, where traditional vernacular features are combined in a more sophisticated fashion. The quite grand dwelling (OPPOSITE) has been allowed to run down slightly – note the distressed state of the whitewash – but has some very interesting architectural features, such as the small staircase to the right, which runs partly outside and partly inside the mass of the building, and the 'Persian' arch, which is pointed at the front and descends to a plain curve at the back. Grander still is this scene (ABOVE) where sophistication borders on the Baroque, with the round window, the juxtaposition of the arches, and the rising curves supporting the stairway on the right. Yet, it is only the finishing detail, not the basic composition, that has changed.

≈ These images, and those on the following pages, come from the beautiful region to the south of Naples. The white villages discussed are Amalfi itself, several smaller locations on the Amalfi Coast (properly described as the Sorrento Peninsula), and Capri, the lovely island off the western tip of the peninsula. This region never came under Arab domination directly, but was once ruled by the Spanish and had extensive trade links with the Arab world. Here, we see the traditional vernacular style dealing with the changing levels and plains by systems of whitewashed stairways (seen in detail, OPPOSITE, BELOW). In the complicated encounters between private access and public thoroughfare (LEFT and OPPOSITE, ABOVE), it is hard to say which is which. There is a sense here that the special quality of vernacular architecture is not so much in the buildings themselves, but in its capacity to cope with the space (or lack of it) between them.

In the small village of Minori (LEFT) the remains of white architecture are few, but here, in a corner built over and around by more recent generations, the sculptural nature of materials and design and the enclosed subterranean atmosphere lead back once more via the *medina* to thoughts of the cave. This is an excellent example of the way in which the whitewashed walls reflect light deep into passages which are barely lit by artificial sources at night, and never during the day. In the complex of passageways in Amalfi (OPPOSITE) the problem of darkness is solved in another way – by boring small apertures through the wall which conduct beams of bright sunlight into the alley. These bounce off the whitewash to produce a highly efficient lighting system, and some remarkable effects. Here, as elsewhere, the vernacular has been much built over: this ancient passageway now serves as a kind of covered-over pavement to the main street, though the old features remain unchanged. Amalfi was a wealthy and powerful trading centre in Medieval times and is sometimes cited as the first maritime power in the world.

≈ RIGHT AND OPPOSITE:
on Capri the old vernacular
architecture has been much
over-built leaving a few
fascinating semi-
subterranean complexes
such as these. The
traditional white buildings
are found hidden at the
bottom of structures which
rise in storeys above them,
their stratifications
telling the age of their
construction like so many
layers in an archaeological
dig. This is the significant
difference between the
vernacular in Italy as
opposed to Spain, Morocco
and the other countries we
look at. Whereas in those
regions the villages are to a
great degree trapped in
time by the lack of any
cultural or commercial
impetus towards
development, the Italian
towns are closer to a
constantly evolving and
changing industrial society
which has inevitably
impacted on their form.
One has to look hard now
for evidence of genuine
white village vernacular,
which is why in this
section, unlike the others,
we are restricted to close-
up images of single streets
rather than townscapes; in
Italy long-distance images,
depicting the top 'crust' of
the town, commonly reveal
little vernacular
architecture.

≈ Capri was well-known to the Romans, and has been continuously inhabited since. Here, the vernacular style seems forced underground by the weight of new building above it. Streets and stairways take the pedestrian through constructions of different epochs; the variety of textures is pleasing and the vernacular areas maintain an authentic atmosphere, with the characteristic elements of whitewashed unity, narrowness and intrigue.

The subterranean
nature of Capri's alleyways
produces some wonderful
effects in the glimpses of
bright streets through long,
dark passages, and the
constantly changing quality
of the light. The practical
need to whiten the risers on
the steps provides, as
elsewhere in Spain and
Greece, an additional
opportunity for decoration.

GREECE

The country, apart from Spain, where white architecture is to be seen at its most developed and at its most attractive is Greece – particularly in the Cyclades Islands and most especially in Amorgos, Mykonos and Santorini. The Greek writer Dimitri Philippides (who edited and contributed the chapter on Santorini in *Greek Traditional Architecture*) does not date Greek vernacular architecture before the fifteenth century; this in itself points to an origin not in the Antique, Hellenistic, Byzantine or Frankish past of these islands but in the time when they were part of the Ottoman Empire. In the sixteenth and seventeenth centuries the Greek subjects of the Ottoman Empire suffered acutely. The Empire itself was in decline, central authority was attenuated, major European powers were making inroads into its commerce with the East, and its resources were drained in unending wars, notably with the Venetians. By the mid-sixteenth century, Mykonos was virtually deserted.

However, the seventeenth century saw a devolution of power by the Turks to their Greek subjects and the eighteenth century was a prosperous one, when a good deal of building took place – building, that is (in these islands at least) in the vernacular style. Traditional building has continued until today. In the resulting townscape, there is no indication in these villages that the buildings belong to one epoch rather than another. It is as if they have been there forever, always pristine white, uninfluenced by the styles and fashions of the outside world.

≈ The sight of bright flowers against white-washed walls (ABOVE) is one of the most evocative vernacular decorative details.

≈ Set on a spectacular site, high above the Aegean, Thira (OPPOSITE), the main village on the island of Santorini (which is also sometimes called Thira), is one of the finest examples of whitewashed vernacular architecture in the whole of the Cyclades. Though beset now with ugly tourist hotels and discotheques, the remnants of what must once have been a truly beautiful old village are still there to be explored and admired. Characteristics of the vernacular form – barrel-vaulted domestic dwellings, domed churches, sculptural staircases – now exist side-by-side with souvenir shops and fast-food outlets. The island is volcanic – created some 80,000 years ago – and has been inhabited since c. BC 2,000, but re-eruptions, the last as recent as 1956, have periodically either wiped out whole communities, or driven them to seek a more amenable situation.

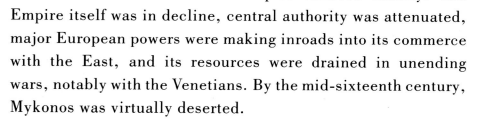

≈ Santorini has been subject to a succession of unfriendly visitors for nearly 2,000 years. Greeks, Egyptians, Macedonians, Venetians, Turks, and Spanish pirates have all, at one time or another, tried their luck at either simple looting or a more formalized conquest. The traditional themes can be detected in the layout of the town around the contours (RIGHT); the narrowness of the streets (which maximize practical use of what flat space is created), and the ever-present whitewash, here seen on both religious and secular structures.

Santorini is a dramatic island. It is a crescent surrounding the cone of a dormant volcano which was formed by a series of devastating eruptions. From the harbour a zig-zag road climbs a steep and rocky slope to Thira, the capital. It receives tourists in large numbers and has been much spoiled by insensitive development. Mykonos on the other hand is also a popular destination, but has absorbed its tourism with much grace. Amorgos is visited less and has, in consequence, a more authentic atmosphere.

≈ This erection (OPPOSITE) is not a shrine or monument, but a traditionally designed chimney sitting on the roof of a dwelling at a lower level.

This beautiful church in Santorini sits high on a hill in the full grandeur of the Mediterranean light. The variety of textures picked out by the sun on the white surfaces is remarkable.

≈ This remarkable tenth-century building – the Monastery of Panayia Khozoviotissa – stands on a spectacular site halfway up an almost vertical, 3,000-foot slope on the island of Amorgos (a comparison with Le Corbusier's Ronchamp chapel has already been drawn). The sea is directly beneath it, and no other building is in sight. On a facade almost wholly devoid of ornament, the articulation of the two massive buttresses is the feature of this building which first catches the eye, and the window-openings also assume a disproportionate significance. The building has no sense of being imposed on the landscape. It appears to grow out of and enrich the setting as much as it is in turn enriched by its location. It is plainly 'man-made', and its form and siting eloquently echo its function to provide a secure and remote sanctuary for prayer and meditation. Local legend tells that a precious icon was cast adrift in a boat by victims of religious persecution in Palestine, and that the people of the island built this monastery to house the relic, directly over the beach where the boat landed. The icon is still there today. Although the building contains fifty rooms and a small church nowhere does the exterior wall of the monastery extend more than twelve feet out from the rock face.

≈ Numerous churches are scattered around the island of Amorgos and these are particularly prevalent, as seen here, in the main village. These delightful vernacular constructions seem to exist around every corner. The four here were photographed on a single route from the periphery to the highest point in the village, on which sits the charming triple church (RIGHT).

≈ Incorporated into the characteristic vernacular repertoire are local Cycladic variations: the picking out of patterns on the floor in white, for example, and the use, as well as of the normal blue, of a second, local colour; a browny-red used on doors and windows since the time of the Turkish occupation. The surface render of the buildings is commonly plaster, but just as often other textures of rock and stone are seen appearing under the whitewash: this mixture of rough and smooth adds much to the aesthetic appearance of the village.

The islands in the Cyclades are liberally dotted with small churches, many of them constructed as thank-offerings by seafarers grateful for a safe return from a hazardous voyage or for a newly-made fortune. Of the churches on Mykonos, this is one of the most ancient and evocative, seeming, like so many of these buildings, to be carved from the land around it rather than separately constructed (see detail of the materials, OPPOSITE). A simple flight of steps leads sideways onto the terrace in front of the entrance, and the arched belfry is handsomely silhouetted against the sky, with a drum behind it, pierced by a small window. This church enjoys a prominent position on the harbour front, where, thanks to the good offices of the watchful local community, no tourist development has been allowed to encroach too closely upon it.

≈ One happy consequence of the attraction of so many tourists is the money they bring with them. The comparative wealth of the town can be seen here, where there is a degree of decoration and embellishment not commonly found elsewhere. All of the basic vernacular characteristics exist – these five street scenes from Mykonos look very similar to those of Frigiliana, for example – but there is a smartness and attention to detail that is not always evident in the poorer vernacular communities. It is, of course, obvious that there is some pressure to maintain standards in order to ensure that the main source of revenue – tourism – is maintained. This decoration, however, works entirely within the vernacular tradition: we are not looking at adaptation or even augmentation so much as enhancement. The flowers are also a common feature in Spain and Italy, as is the picking out of highlights – windows, doors, balconies and so on – in red and blue: but here, amidst the relative richness of the seaside vernacular, everything is 'just so' and 'more so'.

≈ It is the tradition in
Mykonos, seen in these two
illustrations, to paint a
pattern on the floor
surface, following the
interstices between the
stones with a wider or
narrower white line.

Most vernacular settlements are built on hillsides, hill-tops or cliffs. Mykonos is a rarity in that it is a genuine sea-side settlement. Although most of what is actually visible here is of recent date, this is the oldest part of the village, and many ancient buildings are integrated into the modern streets. The people of Mykonos have a reputation for openness and friendliness, and have not allowed the seasonal rigours of the tourist invasion to harden or embitter them (as has happened to the inhabitants of other beauty spots in the Aegean and elsewhere). The local community shows a great concern for the integrity of the town's architecture. It is interesting to see how streets hidden beneath the weight of endless displays of cheap souvenirs and beachwear during the high season are miraculously revealed as simple rows of vernacular buildings when the last holidaymakers have left.

ELEMENTS OF THE MEDITERRANEAN VERNACULAR

≈ OPPOSITE: this typical scene in Mykonos is formed from the characteristic elements of vernacular architecture analyzed in this chapter: the familiar steps and the usual narrow streets; the ubiquitous whiteness and variety in texture; and additional colour and decorative features. The whole is set off by the patterns of light and shade under the Mediterranean sun. BELOW: a detail of the traditional local pavement design of Mykonos.

When viewing these traditional vernacular villages and towns from different countries, what immediately strikes the eye is the consistency among them. Whatever the geographical location, it is plain that each is essentially developed and formed from the same components. Up until now, we have looked at the vernacular tradition with reference to its occurrence in particular countries, but in order fully to appreciate its continuity throughout the Mediterranean basin, it is also necessary, and fascinating, to compare examples from the different areas thematically. In the following pages we have drawn together images to illustrate these architectural similarities in the region as a whole.

The origin of this common style is uncertain, though we can make some relatively assured assumptions. Clearly it was heavily influenced by building methods and forms which were brought into the region and generally spread by the Moorish invasions we have described. Just as obviously, these techniques and other construction methods would have freely circulated in the region through the busy trade routes and the natural movement between populations. The growing similarity between the architecture in the various countries would then have evolved as natural selection gradually promoted the adoption of the most efficient building technology.

● *Siting*

But there may be more to the story than this. Local architecture undoubtedly existed before the arrival of the Arabs, and what had previously existed may have been only influenced, rather than totally reconstructed, by their customs. It is interesting to speculate that components of the vernacular style may to a large degree already have developed independently in the different countries – evolving from natural solutions to the problems of siting, climate, and the availability of materials, which, as these were fundamentally the same in each place, could have produced essentially the same results in each region. Such a hypothesis would certainly explain the way in which the settlements are integrated so organically with their landscapes – one of the features which has done so much to ensure their longevity, charm and architectural success.

≈ Amalfi

The first priority when founding a village is to ensure the availability of food and water. In these vernacular villages the problem of food was solved by siting the community near good agricultural land or close to the sea, and water would be sought from springs or rivers. But in times when the threat of invasion was constant, and when, even in relatively peaceful periods, the community might be subject to attack by marauding bands of outlaws or pirates (or even hungry neighbouring settlements), it was pointless to locate the settlement comfortably close to a rich source of sustenance if it left it vulnerable. It is for this reason that the majority of these vernacular villages were sited on rocky outcrops, cliffs, or high in the hills where attackers would find it difficult, if not impossible, to overcome them and steal their supplies. The fact that defence was as important as access to food and water in the siting of a settlement is proven by the existence of many hill villages that have no direct access to water – they preferred the discomfort of fetching and storing water to insecurity. Hill-top sites were favoured not only for defensive purposes, but also because they allowed maximum utilization of all the flat agricultural land available.

The result is the magnificent hillside architecture seen here (at Casares, top right; at Almunecar, bottom right; and at Amalfi, left) and elsewhere in the book, where fortified buildings sit proudly on hilltops, and dwellings seem to hang from cracks in the rock, or to be cascading down the cliffside towards the sea.

Not all whitewashed towns and villages are found on hilltop sites. In Competa, Spain (bottom far right), for example, the inhabitants have been tempted down closer to the fertile plain. Given that the occupants felt that proximity to their crops could override the need for security, it is likely that the community was founded in more tranquil times.

≈ Casares

≈ Almunecar

≈ Competa

≈ 117

● *Contours*

If it were possible to lift one of these towns off the landscape to examine the ground beneath, one would see a series of terraces cut into the hillside like giant cylindrical steps which, where they go all the way around the hill, grow smaller and smaller in circumference as they ascend. Some of these step-terraces can be seen uncovered in Frigiliana (middle far right). These building terraces are not formally organized and created around the contours of the hill before the building of the settlement commences: they have been randomly shaped over the centuries as somebody chooses a plot and roughly flattens it in order to build level with the neighbouring property. Sometimes the streets are not level at all, but wind up the hill at an angle, sometimes gently, sometimes steeply. Often the new construction will not even adopt the contour line, but will be fashioned counter to it, perhaps fitting itself into and spanning the gap between houses on two separate levels, or even taking its place in a steep street running altogether against the contour-lines so that each dwelling has to be individually levelled within. On this page are illustrated some examples of shifting levels within towns in Spain, Greece and Italy.

 Frigiliana

≈ Mykonos

≈ Frigiliana

≈ Frigiliana

≈ Sperlonga

● *Changing Levels and Steps*

With the split-level townscape goes the stepped street, which, in the opportunity it presents for enhanced decoration of the ground plan and the ever-changing viewpoint it creates for the pedestrian, can transform otherwise undistinguished rows of domestic housing into interesting, charming and distinctive thoroughfares.

The *ad hoc* building solutions that have evolved over generations to the problems caused by the choice of sloping sites are one of the most fascinating and intriguing elements of the study of vernacular architecture. An elaborate, but random, infrastructure of landings, walkways and staircases is developed in each community to allow movement between and access to the different levels as they form. As has been noted before, it is the handling of these spaces between the buildings, almost as much as the buildings themselves, which lies at the heart of this architectural tradition. The images on this and the following page, again from Italy, Spain and Greece, show variations, but above all similarities, in the regional treatment of this element.

≈ Mykonos

≈ Frigiliana

≈ Sperlonga

≈ Frigiliana

≈ Sperlonga

●*N a r r o w   S t r e e t s*

≈ Frigiliana

This effect is found everywhere in the Mediterranean basin. It is perhaps more understandable in the hill villages, where the dwellings hug either side of the level, narrow terraces, yet it is also prevalent in flatter towns and seems to be a natural feature of cultures which flourish in close proximity. These settlements grew organically, and some of the 'closeness' of the architecture is related to the extension of family groups – as a dowry for a newly married daughter, a house was built on to the side of or opposite the family home. In addition, the house groups were tightly formed, rather like the archetypal wagon ring, for better defence and security. The climate also plays a role, in the desire for the shade these streets provide; and siting, too, in that living a little closer to a neighbour is a small price to pay for greater use of available agricultural land. The resulting effect of all these dynamics is a wonderful range of architecturally fascinating and aesthetically delightful streets such as those illustrated on this page from Italy, Tunisia, Spain, Morocco and Greece, and overleaf, from Sperlonga in Italy.

≈ Mykonos

≈ Chaouen

≈ Amalfi

≈ Hammamet

≈ Sperlonga

≈ Amorgos

≈ Minori

● *Enclosed Streets*

Tunnel architecture and enclosed passageways grew
naturally from the narrow streets. Where the
geographical constraints forced construction
upwards, the lower levels, where the authentic
white vernacular buildings are still evident, often
became overbuilt. Arches, originally designed to
buttress upper storeys, spread and, perhaps joining
on to buildings and footbridges on higher levels,
eventually created complexes of fully enclosed
passageways, reminiscent, as previously noted, of
troglodyte networks where all architecture began.
These examples show some stages of this
development: an arch with a dwelling above it in
Morocco (below); similar effects in Greece (far left)
and Italy (top left); and actual tunnel areas in
Tunisia (right) and Italy (bottom left). Here, again,
the trans-regional similarities are obvious.

≈ Hammamet

≈ Chaouen

● *Decoration*

Prosperity, of course, has two faces. In some instances wealth is used to maintain the existing architecture and its features impeccably, as evidenced by the red and green paintwork on the elegant traditional wooden balustrades of Mykonos. In other cases it gives the owner the option to make 'improvements' on the style, by the use of bought-in materials such as tiles and wrought-iron-work, and by introducing elements such as exterior lighting or decorative devices such as new colour-schemes and patterns. The impulse to replace simple traditional features with jazzy imports (as seen in the orange iron-work in Mykonos, top far right) is not restricted to elaborations on the Mediterranean vernacular – it is a common theme in the history of all architectural disciplines. Where wealth is available the temptation to change and experiment is strong; and the principal lesson here may be that the uniformity of style in the Mediterranean vernacular has been preserved and reinforced over the generations by a conjunctive absence of privilege. Seen here are examples of decorative elements *within* the vernacular tradition, from Morocco, Greece and Spain.

≈ Chaouen

≈ Mykonos

≈ Mykonos

≈ Frigiliana

≈ Frigiliana

≈ Mykonos

≈ Mykonos

≈ Mykonos

≈ Sperlonga

≈ Amalfi

≈ Minori

● *L i g h t*

Le Corbusier said, in *Towards a New Architecture*, 'Architecture is the masterly, correct and magnificent play of masses brought together in light'. Surely no region in the world is blessed with richer and more dramatic light than these Mediterranean countries. It is the final intangible element in this whitewashed vernacular tradition, taking an already special form, and displaying it as something altogether extraordinary. The sunlight picking out the hundreds of textures in the vernacular villages imbues them with a tactile quality not found in other architectural traditions, and its interplay with the universal whitewash is both visually and aesthetically dazzling. At the same time this vernacular style just as commonly makes a feature of the virtual absence of light. The architectural composition of the narrow, shade-inducing streets, semi-subterranean passageways, tunnels and vaults is completed by a light which is so heavily filtered and altered that it appears to take on the colour and substance of the building fabric around it. On this page an example from Tunisia illustrates the glamour of a building shining in the full Mediterranean light, while more romantic images from Italy and Tunisia show some of the effects that filtered light can create. Overleaf, a mosque on Djerba is perhaps paradigmatic of the quotation which opens this page.

≈ Houmt Souk

≈ Ksar Haddada

THE INFLUENCE OF THE VERNACULAR

≈

"(The vernacular) does not go through fashion cycles. It is real, immutable, indeed unimprovable, since it serves its purpose to perfection."

BERNARD RUDOFSKY

THE VERNACULAR DEFINED

Our appreciation of the Mediterranean vernacular, as we have seen, derives from a series of strong images gathered while walking the streets, stopping in the small square or climbing the next hillside to look back at the village; images which are rounded out when we study these photographs or our own humble snaps and sketches long after the visit. The composite impressions lead us to talk of 'effortless style', 'organic pattern' or even 'timeless quality' in our attempt to define what we have seen, but such phrases do not capture the essence of these settlements. Nor do they define the qualities which could inform and inspire the design of new settlements or the conservation of what is already there.

The alternative approach, followed below, is to analyze these habitats as a designer might describe his own new project. What are the specific architectural qualities to be found there? Which, for a fellow designer, would command respect and admiration? To analyze them in this way does not destroy their freshness or pin them like some prize butterfly into a display cabinet. Nor can it replace the first-hand experience of the scent of fresh flowers in the oil can vases or the sounds of villages coming alive in the morning.

Of course talking of these small towns in terms of 'design themes' can impose a self-conscious, knowing gloss on what are clearly traditional usages and practices. If we use contemporary design phraseology in our attempts to analyze and define the qualities we admire in these vernacular settlements we do so only as a convenience, a shorthand.

≈ Breaking down the vernacular style of a street such as this (OPPOSITE) in Mykonos into components for analysis can produce many valuable lessons for contemporary architects. At the same time it cannot replace actual experience of the living environment: the charm and success of the effect produced by this cameo of window and flowers on Paros (LEFT) is almost indefinable, and certainly unrepeatable in other architectural forms.

≈ Ralph Erskine's East Anglian drainpipes make a feature of a climatic event, rather than understating it. The anonymous builders of the vernacular adopted a similarly aesthetic response to the challenges of the climate, but with much less self-consciousness.

Climatic Sense and Functional Fitness

We can begin with building details intended to solve the problems of climate. Creative architects have often built their architecture around climatic imperatives, celebrating the particular character of the local climate in the design of their buildings. In the Middle East, certain contemporary architects have built projects around the need to create comfortable conditions in the harsh desert climate. The most notable of these projects must be the new Ministry of Foreign Affairs in Riyadh, Saudi Arabia, by the Danish architect Henning Larsen, in which shaded internal courtyards recall the tradition of the desert oasis. The English architect Ralph Erskine, who has worked in Sweden for half a century, has drawn inspiration from the extremes of climate. Working in Cambridge for the new postgraduate community of Clare Hall, Erskine designed a 'ski-slope' roofscape that ends in gigantic, over-scaled rainwater downpipes discharging into huge drains to remind us that East Anglia can be rather wet for much of the year. In Sweden, he has produced a series of settlement designs for the far north, in which the architectural detailing — hence much of the visual interest — is derived directly from the functional need to detach elements of structure, such as external balconies, from the main body of the building to avoid heat loss. While this 'climatic architecture' can easily become a New Romanticism in itself, it is no more fashionable and superficial than tile hoods over village windows in Morocco or Spain, as described below. Both make excellent functional sense, and if in the process they also embellish the building, then so much the better.

Spanish and Moroccan hill villages often contain projections over windows which protect the opening below from the winter rain and from the bright sun of spring and summer. These horizontal ledges are formed very simply from a double row of Roman tiles, the lower row inverted to hold the mortar. Sometimes this mini-roof covers a projecting ledge built back into

≈ The vernacular form is so consistently simple that any divergence from the norm becomes an event. Texture takes on a disproportionate significance, whether it is deliberately intended by the builder to become a 'feature', or whether the effect is purely accidental. The range of textures created is endless: seen here are a pavement in Santorini (ABOVE); an undecorated stone wall in Ibiza (ABOVE RIGHT); and, more exotically, a mud fortress in southern Morocco (RIGHT).

top of wall, resulting in a composite elevation which is not only appealing in picturesque terms but also offers an instant biography of the dwelling.

These textural contrasts are at the most extreme in the Greek Islands, where hillside sites have been terraced to remove the minimum of rock, leaving outcrops of exposed material as street elevations, which are then whitewashed. In the Italian and Spanish hillside villages, textural contrasts are formed by successive periods of masonry construction, as some owners upgrade their properties with more prestigious materials alongside their neighbours who do nothing. The textures are heightened by the all-pervading whiteness, so that there are smooth whites, whites with varying degrees of roughness and whites with regular patterning. This textural play can be noted in the work of many Modern architects with Mediterranean connections. Alvar Aalto, for example, often composed wall surfaces with overlapping textures of white-painted slatted boards or brickwork, render and treated concrete.

Concentrated Detail

One of the greatest attractions of the vernacular architecture of the Mediterranean is the play of detail against mass. The proportion of visible openings to solid wall will often be small, with mass dominating door- and window-openings. There is never any uncertainty as to whether the building is a frame filled in with solid panels or predominantly a solid with openings cut in. The buildings-as-sculpture theme is an important element in the continuing appeal of these vernacular settlements to 'sophisticated' western designers. As Le Corbusier himself writes in his manifesto *Towards a New Architecture,* 'Architecture is the masterly, correct and magnificent play of masses brought together in light'. What more magnificent masses can be imagined than those of the Greek Island villages climbing rocky hillsides, or the shining settlements of the Maghreb?

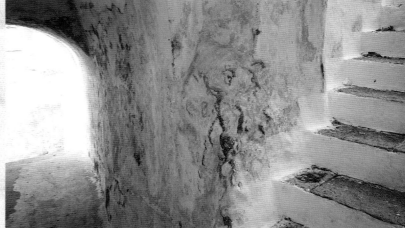

≈ The basic similarities of materials and approach produce a consistency of rich textures throughout the Mediterranean. The effects illustrated here come from a subterranean street in Minori (ABOVE), and from churches in Ibiza (OPPOSITE, and LEFT); while the background texture is a plastered, whitewashed wall in the Greek Island style.

Since mass always predominates – a pattern of white masonry walls, continuous surfaces and limited openings – areas of detail such as windows, door and balconies gain emphasis because they are viewed against a calm, neutral background (though it would be stretching a point to argue that the Mediterranean vernacular always includes such a self-conscious, knowing composition of plain wall backgrounds in the sense that a window-dresser might set sophisticated jewellery on a background of forest bark to better display its beauty). This contrasts with the visual anarchy of much modern architecture, which is often little more than an unthinking assembly of catalogue building products arranged side by side. Since there was no functional justification for large openings, and in any event these would be difficult and expensive to construct with the building methods locally available, an automatic feature of the Mediterranean vernacular is the background as a foil for building features.

Such features can be very modest in size, perhaps a single casement window with its shutters, but still prove visually effective when set in the predominant background of a whitewashed wall. There is always sufficient solid area for these details to register, just as an artist might lead the eye to the most important points on his canvas by locally increasing the level of decorative detail and ornamentation.

≈ The street in Frigiliana (OPPOSITE) is a classic example of new architecture being added to old in the authentic vernacular style. The wall on the left is formed of living rock at the base, which supports the upper terrace, allowing building on the outer edge of the lower terrace. The different textures in the rock wall, which is raised and finished at the top with a plastered layer, tell the story of the village's development like the strata in an archaeological dig. ABOVE: the predominating mass of white means that even the smallest colour detail becomes a major decorative event.

Windows

One of the most familiar components of the Mediterranean vernacular is the window: its simple functional purpose of controlling light and ventilation to the room within belies its value as a canvas on which the personality of the owner can be expressed. Windows come many-layered, with their external shutters, ventilation screens, and sometimes iron grills set forward of the wall plane. They reflect the various demands put upon the window-opening – security, privacy, air movement or outlook. Varying in sophistication from the simplest

≈ The rather effective decoration on this window (ABOVE) is provided by leaving the protruding stones which surround and support the window-opening unwhitened. From the middle distance (RIGHT) the three elements which combine to create the impression of the townscape are the white building cubes, the red sloping roofs, and the punctuation of the tiny window apertures.

Cycladian 'hole in the wall' opening to the elegant veils of layering seen in the larger Spanish or Moroccan villages (where status and prosperity play their part) these functional elements of the window can produce in combination a rich wholeness of their own. This has been echoed, for example, in recent Spanish architecture, which often borrows the window

proportions and layering of planes from the vernacular to produce wall elevations of great elegance and climatic appropriateness. Buildings such as the recent headquarters for the Previsíon Español in Seville are carefully composed to contrast massive areas of brickwork sympathetic to the adjacent city walls with finely detailed sunscreens and shutters protecting deep-set window-openings.

As in the village architecture of Spain, windows can be given greater emphasis by bringing them forward of the main wallplane, framing them with applied mouldings or crowning them with protective hoods. A single house will display a hierarchy of openings, some diminished in importance and others given greater emphasis. Again, this is a formal device found throughout the history of architecture.

Balconies
A further glory of the Mediterranean vernacular, balconies share in the life of the street, often projecting at first floor level like the boxes of an opera house, or forming a threshold

≈ The 'hole in the wall' window-opening with a wooden shutter, as seen (ABOVE LEFT) in Mykonos, is the simplest and most common form in this vernacular architecture: as has been seen opposite, occasionally a very basic form of ornamentation is created (ABOVE) by leaving the stone or brick window surround in its natural colour.

≈ The window aperture is one of the few opportunities for decoration and personal statement on the otherwise uniformly white mass of the vernacular dwelling. Whereas in the vast majority of cases ornament is limited, both by poverty and by the conservative nature of these settlements, where it does occur, and is kept within the vernacular context, window-dressing provides a notable break in the rhythm of the settlement's architecture. The iron-work (FAR RIGHT) is a local tradition in the Chaouen *medina*, and the more elaborate Italian shutters (OPPOSITE) are merely a development out of a functional response to a climatic necessity. It is interesting to compare similar effects from vernacular architecture on the fringes of the Mediterranean style: the curved iron-work and windowbox from the Cote d'Azur (ABOVE RIGHT) would not look out of place in Spain, and the Portuguese wooden half-grill (BELOW RIGHT) clearly has an Islamic heritage.

platform at an upper entry. They provide ready opportunities for the proud display of plants and possessions within a defined private territory safe from passers-by. Typically formed in wood in the Greek Islands, or in iron-work in Italy and Spain, they establish a linear pattern contrasting with the plainness of the wall behind. They often form the basis for a semi-enclosed outdoor room, open to the sky and swathed in planting. This framework serves as an intermediate space between the public street and the privacy of the dwelling, much as the traditional Islamic *mashrabiya* (oriel window), still seen in Jeddah or Cairo, will protect the womenfolk within but allow them views down to the street below.

Balconies provide the extrovert alternative to the private courtyards within the house, promoting outdoor living and social activity. They have always proved attractive to designers as functional elements which can lend 'instant' identity to a dwelling and differentiate it from its neighbours, particularly in the case of mass housing. Alvar Aalto and Ralph Erskine are the two architects whose enthusiasm for the design and social potential of the balcony is most apparent. In both cases they were very familiar with the Mediterranean vernacular. Louis Kahn has also developed balconies as a key element, whether for research scientists to contemplate the cosmos, as in his Salk Institute in La Jolla, California, overlooking the Pacific, or for young students to compose their thoughts, as in his college dormitories at Bryn Mawr, Pennsylvania.

≈ The balcony is a common feature in the architecture of the region: this one in Mykonos (RIGHT) forms both an outdoor living area and a first floor opening allowing communication over an informal meeting space. Le Corbusier was inspired to include a similar first floor projection at Ronchamp (ABOVE).

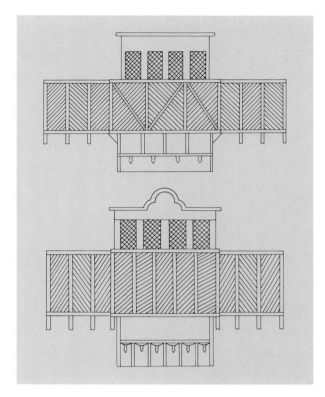

≈ In the vernacular architecture of the Middle East the *mashrabiya*, or oriel window (ABOVE RIGHT) serves as an enclosed balcony that allows the women of the family discreetly to view the street below. It is a device which has been used somewhat unfortunately by contemporary architects in the region, both to cover external ducts, and as a rather unimaginative decorative pastiche. An authentic oriel window in Syria (BELOW) shows the elegance and effectiveness of the feature in its proper context. Louis Kahn appreciated the functional versatility of the balcony, employing it (ABOVE) in the Salk Institute project at La Jolla, California.

Celebrated Thresholds

Whether in Greece, Spain or the Maghreb, the point of entry to each dwelling receives proper emphasis and attention. This celebration of the threshold is a familiar objective of contemporary architects, especially if they are involved in the design of public-sector housing, where identity is all too easily subsumed in the sheer number of units. In the vernacular examples illustrated in this volume, this identity is achieved in many apparently effortless ways, all within the context of the visual unity of the settlement as a whole. The house threshold can be defined by a slight change of level – perhaps a single step, a small ledge to one side of a sloping street on which the visitor can pause before entering in at the front door, a recess in the wallplane which defines and shelters the doorway, or by a flight of steps leading to the main entrance at first floor level. These devices can be reinforced by whitewashed trim to the steps or modulations in the texture of the stone pavement. Surrounded by the all-embracing whiteness, these inflections of the threshold, although achieved with the simplest of architectural means, make the transition between the public realm of the street and the private world of the dwelling with consummate ease. Modern designers might learn useful lessons here. It is a problem which has been solved successfully in the best public housing projects in Europe, by architects such as Edward Cullinan, Richard MacCormac and Darboure and Darke in Britain, Aldo van Eyck in Holland, and Robert Venturi in America.

≈ Doors, as windows, provide a rare break in the white mass of the structure, and another opportunity for decoration. This can take many forms: seen here are the door to a Tunisian mosque (LEFT); the entrance to an Ibizan church (BELOW); and a painted door surround on a Greek church (OPPOSITE, BELOW). It is interesting to compare typical doorways in whitewashed vernacular dwellings in Cyprus (OPPOSITE, LEFT) and southern Portugal (OPPOSITE, RIGHT).

Infrastructure

Viewed from above, Mediterranean villages seem to be sculptured or quarried from a single block of stone. Unified by their pervasive whiteness they are traversed by streets and passageways which appear as deep gouges into the mass as they subdivide the islands of buildings. Closer study reveals that this pattern of routes has been determined by a combination of functional factors: by historic land ownership, by the lie of the site, by the predetermined location of major buildings, and by the need to link public places, bridge crossings, defensive strongpoints, harbours or routes from the hinterland. Others were decided by the position of ancient tracks now solidified in stone. Climate is also a formative influence: streets can be orientated for maximum shading of pedestrians and exposed walls of dwellings, or where appropriate, to offer protection from hostile winds.

≈ Observed from a distance these settlements (here Cefalu in Sicily, ABOVE) are so dense that, although breaks in the mass of the townscape may be detected, it is almost impossible to identify any system of streets or through routes. It is only on closer examination that the basic infrastructure of the settlement begins to become evident. As in Mykonos (RIGHT) streets have evolved over hundreds of years, their routes set by ancient land boundaries, random building, and the positioning of major structures such as churches. For what are quite small communities, the complexity of the townscape is extraordinary, operating as it does on multiple levels, with little differentiation between public and private spaces, until, at a highly localized level, a route will finally drift into an alley giving access to an individual dwelling, or a private courtyard such as this one in Spain (OPPOSITE).

While these functional considerations will determine the broad framework of routes, at the local level they are always subject to those minor quirks of alignment which add so much to their appeal. Many of these are clearly accidental – the result of property disputes and land assembly over the centuries – but others show a definite intention to form a larger public space where the route is widened out. The main 'river' of space flows on, with small side 'eddies' and setbacks of the facade-plane providing emphasis at entrances or the opportunity to set out a round of chairs or preserve a pair of olive trees. This book contains many examples of such happy incidents that could not have been generated by any number of design guidelines.

≈ These ancient *ghorfas* in southern Tunisia (ABOVE), with their honeycomb network of work spaces, seem to be only one step away from true cave dwellings. Their multiple barrel-vaulted structure might well have provided the inspiration for Louis Kahn's Kimbell Art Museum project at Forth Worth, Texas (OPPOSITE, LEFT).

Return to the Cave

Certain vernacular forms can be traced back to the troglodytic dwellings quarried into the soft rock of island hillsides such as those of Santorini in the southern Cyclades. Certainly, the cave-like internal spaces of many freestanding vernacular houses reinforce this hypothesis. In these buildings, especially public ones such as storehouses, churches, mosques and markets, may be found complex, labyrinthine volumes formed by masonry piers that recall those natural stone pillars which remained after the excavation of storage chambers in the hillside. The power of these interiors has few parallels in the legacy of Modern architecture with the distinguished exception of the later work of Louis Kahn. Throughout his long career Kahn continued to create powerful masonry masses with brick-built piers and shallow arches that have an undatable aura of strength. In perhaps his finest mature work – the Indian Institute of Management at Ahmedabad (1962–1974) – he used brickwork with great virtuosity, not for its own sake but to form huge window reveals, vaulted spaces and layered interiors that were especially powerful under the sharp light of the subcontinent. While never a prisoner of the vernacular, Kahn created columned spaces which are as timeless as the caverns of Santorini; his window-openings also echoed historic precedent in their use of semicircular forms, often with a tie beam on the chord and a narrow vertical opening centred below.

The place of 'vernacular' vaults in the work of Le Corbusier has already been noted in reference to Tunisia. The barrel vault form is also commonly found in the Greek Island settlements, taking its place alongside other prismatic solids as an important building block in the overall composition of these villages, and frequently occurring as part of larger, non-domestic buildings such as churches and chapels. A return to simple unadorned geometric solids in architecture was favoured by Le Corbusier as a re-affirmation of fundamental sculptural values. Such geometry is commonly found in the buildings and

≈ These ancient houses in Medinine, Morocco (RIGHT), are barely advanced in shape and texture from cave dwellings. The illustration (BELOW RIGHT) shows the design of a typical troglodyte system, with the final shape of the living spaces being totally dependent on the softness and workability of the rock. Louis Kahn actually designed a whole complex – the Indian Institute of Management at Ahmedabad – on the theme of a cave dwelling.

building groups of the Mediterranean, where their use was not so much a matter of aesthetic preference but rather the direct consequence of the need for simple, robust and economic structural systems, which could then be embellished by local decorative accents without diluting their power. What is undeniable is the continuing appeal to sophisticated architectural palates of such primal solids and volumes, unified by their dressing of whitewash and bathed in Mediterranean light.

THE ARCHITECT AND THE VERNACULAR

≈ The church at Santa Eulalia, Ibiza (OPPOSITE) is typical of the problems that vernacular buildings present to the architectural academic. Once a mosque, now a Christian church, it has evolved over the years in reaction to historical and political developments, and in response to the community's requirements, with a number of different additions, including work by a classical Italian architect, Calvi. The resulting structure is almost impossible to describe in the normal architectural vocabulary. Primitive types such as this dwelling in Guadix, Andalusia (BELOW), similarly elude academic categorization.

Architectural morphology – the theory of architectural form – is an inexact and contentious science. Vernacular settlements do not fit neatly into its predetermined categories. Indeed, as Bernard Rudofsky notes in the introduction to his pioneering discussion of the vernacular, *Architecture Without Architects*, the academic study of architectural history is highly selective. 'It skips the bucolic and heroic stages of architecture's small hours, and presents instead a bewildering catalogue of monumental minutiae, generously asterisked and dragging the ball and chain of footnotes.' What he calls 'pedigreed architecture' has grabbed centre stage in the textbooks and lecture theatres, to the exclusion of the great mass of building that has no designer label attached.

Rudofsky scores a palpable hit. For all the sophistication of research methods, information sources and jet-lagged academics, architectural history has not broadened its scope beyond the orderly ranking and description of buildings and their designers. Banister-Fletcher, whose *History of Architecture on the Comparative Method* (1896) was still being reprinted as a standard textbook for architectural students in the 1960s, would feel thoroughly at home with current architectural historians; only the names of the architects have been changed to reflect intervening developments in architecture.

Vernacular architecture does not suit the celebrity architect and the 'seminal building' approach at all. There are no ready labels to pin onto what appears to be a unified but anonymous structure. Instead, the would-be critic has to resort to the unsatisfactory language of tourism in an attempt to capture the architectural qualities of Mediterranean settlements. It is rare to find any sustained urban design analysis of a village in terms of its spatial composition, street pattern, building form and constituent architecture. If found, such material leans towards archaeology, anthropology or sociology rather than architecture.

Nonetheless, the vernacular, including the Mediterranean white villages, is used in architectural polemics to signal a return to what are promoted as basic architectonic values: the cubic white masses and patterns of solid and void. These 'values' are of continuing appeal to contemporary architects. In considering this it could be argued that there is an un-acknowledged element of patronage or inverted snobbery in such an endorsement of vernacular design. Just as Le Corbusier puts engineers on a pedestal, claiming that 'The Engineer, inspired by the law of Economy and governed by mathematical calculation, puts us in accord with universal law. He achieves harmony', so can the vernacular builders be apotheosized. To praise them is to wear an open-necked shirt and not the stuffy smock of an architectural atelier. Louis Kahn, the American master architect, similarly addressed a conference in Iran as follows:

> *Now, if you think that the villager is not using art, then you are greatly mistaken, because it is the true language of man. There is no other language, nothing is truer, because it is that part which contains the most intangible, therefore it is truer to man, because man is essentially born of the intangible and he is only using the tangible to express himself, nothing more.*

≈ Louis Kahn tried hard to recapture the spontaneity of the true vernacular in the Kimbell Art Museum (OPPOSITE): but many contemporary architects, while affecting vernacular influences, are in fact drawing from more sophisticated sources, such as this traditional house in Granada (LEFT), to reinterprete the form in a prettified, cottage *orné* style.

The vernacular builders were thus idealized as untutored designers free from the taint of the academic architectural education that so bedevilled their benighted contemporaries.

If we extend the Rudofsky argument, it appears that vernacular builders are somehow imbued with what appears to be a 'generic' case approach — following sets of rules which determine each turn of the wall or the set of each window — without recourse to formal instruction or any conscious aesthetic. Many of these rules or principles will have their origins, presumably, in sound building practice, available materials, local technology and so on. To our connoisseur's eye, the outcome is attractive and memorable, but is this not also the case with items from the natural world — rock formations, spiral shells, DNA molecules or cross-sections of a fly's eye? All these 'products' could be called functional, in that they successfully resolve the various constraints in the shaping of an object, be it natural or manmade. In the case of Mediterranean vernacular, there can only be a limited number of ways of forming a window or door opening in a masonry wall without importing a new technology such as reinforced concrete. It is

≈ The barrel-vaulted structures in Tunisia (OPPOSITE) and Mykonos (BELOW) are simple forms to fulfil basic functions. Conservatism maintained the vernacular almost unchanged for centuries, while in northern Europe architects were experimenting with ever-more ambitious structures, such as the Gothic cathedrals. The nave in the magnificent cathedral of Beauvais (RIGHT) stands as a monument to the ingenuity, imagination, and perseverance of the builders of the late Middle Ages. It took centuries to construct, collapsed several times during the process, and is today held together internally by a network of iron tie-rods, while flying buttresses in three tiers of immense thickness take the thrust of the vault externally.

not surprising, therefore, that these openings are comparably proportioned throughout the village settlements.

If we turn to the writings of the French architect and theorist Auguste Choisy at the turn of the century, we find a reasoned explanation for architectural form which argues that whatever the case, the (structural) solution is the direct outcome of a correct definition of the problem. *'La question posée, la solution etait indiquée'*, wrote Choisy in his *Histoire de l'Architecture* (1899), building upon an analysis of architectural history that had been initiated earlier by Durand and Viollet-le-Duc. Whether describing the evolution of the Greek temple or the Gothic vault, Choisy argued that structural solutions imposed themselves once the problem had been correctly stated. Self-conscious art did not come into the picture. This argument is taken up later by, amongst others, the English architect W. R. Lethaby. Speaking to the Architectural Association in London in 1915, he declared, 'A fine fishing rod, a well-tuned fiddle, have their just proportions; and Gothic architecture was developed not by any aesthetic view of the proportions, but by getting the nerved vault, the ramping buttress and the stone-barred window to do the utmost possible.'

This functional view of how buildings came to be the way they are would seem to find support in vernacular settlements, where solutions to the practical problems of shelter, storage, available building technology and climate had to be found. But there is one important difference. In both cases – the need to support ever-more extensive areas of glass high in a cathedral nave, or to vault over an island storehouse with locally available stone – a core problem can be identified: yet the history of Gothic architecture in Europe, for example, is one of experiment, occasional dramatic failures, and continuing evolution, whereas the history of the vernacular is near static, retaining construction methods and usages that often include a large measure of structural redundancy. 'Build now as you have always built' appears to be the rule.

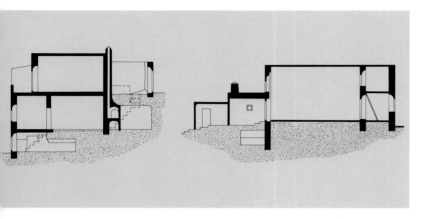

≈ This plan shows the very simple solutions developed by vernacular builders to the problem of constructing two and three storey dwellings on sloping sites. This system has not changed for centuries; because their needs never vary, there is no need for these communities to reach out for new techniques.

Rudofsky acknowledges, even rejoices in this static state. In the passage already quoted he describes the vernacular as 'nearly immutable', and further contrasts 'the serenity of the architecture in so-called underdeveloped countries with the architectural blight in industrial countries'. After all, if the 'problem' does not change over the centuries because it is a simple problem that can be easily solved — such as forming a small opening in a masonry wall or roofing a modest room — then there is no great incentive to search beyond time-honoured and proven techniques and materials. The innate conservatism of vernacular architecture can be acknowledged, not as a mark of rebuke but as a self-evident statement confirmed by detailed analysis of any Mediterranean village.

The difficulty arises when circumstances change, the problems change and traditional solutions cannot cope. There can be nothing less convincing, for example, than attempts to resurrect vernacular methods of construction to build a new tourist complex in or adjacent to an existing village, not that this exercise has not been boldly attempted. Certainly, most Modern architectural attempts to re-use vernacular features, such as a *mashrabiya* used to screen exposed airconditioning units in the Middle East, have proved artistically unfortunate.

On the other hand the architect Hassan Fathy's lifelong experiments with the building methods and forms of the Egyptian vernacular have yielded ensembles of undoubted authenticity, such as his famous village of New Gournah, on the west bank of the Nile facing Luxor. It remains largely uninhabited, the consequences of political naïvety rather than any shortfall in its conception and design. But to reactivate the traditions and skills of mud-brick building in this way required both a lifetime of persistence in the face of official disdain and a distinguished architect's ability to analyze and then re-invent the whole culture of mud construction. Ironically, Fathy has received more recognition for his vernacular theories outside his native land than within it.

≈ Vernacular houses in Luxor (ABOVE) where Hassan Fathy devoted his life to projects inspired by mud-form dwellings. The barrel vault (PLAN, TOP) is the vernacular building technique most commonly borrowed by modern architects.

INFLUENCES: THE LIVING TRADITION

As favoured destinations of the architectural élite, vernacular settlements in the Mediterranean have served the dual function of offering respite from and inspiration for project development. Since the last century, architect-travellers to the Mediterranean have continued to bring back souvenirs in the

form of urban prototypes and aesthetic preferences which they have then proceeded to recreate in their own work. Much of the appeal undoubtedly lies in the memories of hot summers in delightful waterside conditions, when day-to-day business is exchanged for leisurely contemplation of architectural values in the company of good wine and friends. Only the most dedicated of designer-pilgrims can know the winter storms and rainswept squares when the Mediterranean vision is dulled and uninviting. When architects sort through their slides, memories and sketches, they do so with the glow of warm beachside evenings still fresh in the mind.

The appeal is undoubtedly strong on contrast. Leaving the urban milieu behind, with its clamour and anonymity, the architect can enjoy a return to first principles. He will probably know little of the traditional culture of the village and fail to appreciate that at times its economy may be in trouble or its inhabitants disenchanted with their lot. Such ignorance only matters when designers try to transplant architectural and urban design ideas culled from their Mediterranean journeys

≈ The Banca Popolare in Verona is a successful example of vernacular 'borrowing' by Carlo Scarpa – placing small window apertures (LEFT) against a brickwork mass. It is understandable that townscapes such as this Spanish scene (OPPOSITE) can inspire contemporary designers to carry home with them seductive ideas about the humanity, sense of community, and tranquillity of these villages: it is only in the inopportune reinterpretation of these concepts that so many unfortunate architectural decisions are made.

directly into different settings. There is nothing as unconvincing or forlorn as a fragment of Santorini transposed to a public housing project in North London or a piece of Paros to Le Corbusier's studio-houses in the Paris of the 1920s.

When viewing the white villages of the Mediterranean in the main section the most striking feature of these vernacular settlements is their location. Most are dense, compact and appear all of a piece when viewed from a distance against a barren background of rock or scrub. They contrast with telling effect with these elemental landscapes, gaining visual tension because they are often only a small feature in the panorama of land, sea and sky. Even in those cases where the surrounding land-forms are unremarkable and indefinite, their sheer extent compared to the compact settlement creates a strong counterpoint and appeal. The villages are powerful because they are homogenous – seemingly sculptured from a single block of material by a single hand. Colour is limited in extent, and the eye is not distracted by competing materials or individually assertive structures, in complete contrast to townscapes in industrialized societies.

The sketchbooks of past architects have always been a valuable quarry from which nineteenth-century designers extracted material for their own eclectic architecture. In this century – the generation of Le Corbusier, Alvar Aalto and Louis Kahn – architects have collected Mediterranean images to support the aesthetic preferences of the emerging Modern movement. Hence the archives of these masters contain a body of sketches which celebrate the sculptural qualities of the Mediterranean vernacular. No matter what the functional and symbolic role of each building group, their articulation or detail was not fully understood in the process of borrowing. Sufficient for them to argue, and not over-rigorously, that the Mediterranean vernacular came about through a process of 'natural' selection and that the result was appealing to the contemporary eye precisely because it had a sound historical basis.

≈ Densely packed housing such as this has originated organically over hundreds of years in places such as Casares. The close-knit grouping of dwellings is accepted by the inhabitants – even welcomed as a fundamental part of their culture. It is misguided in the extreme to think that similar groupings can be casually recreated in other cultural environments as an easy solution to mass housing requirements.

The visual impact of the homogenous whitewashed village is paralleled closely in architects' models, which follow the convention of a single colour, usually matt white, as a means of emphasizing the basic form of the proposal without the distractions of colour, texture or material. For example, the Finnish master architect Alvar Aalto filled his atelier in Munkeniemi near Helsinki with white-sprayed plywood models of his current projects. Aalto's site models presented buildings, road and landscape in a single unified style: everything was white, crisp and sculptural. Besides being a convention of presentation that owed much to the Beaux Arts tradition in architecture, the 'white style' certainly recalled the 1933 summer trip Aalto made to the CIAM (Congrès Internationaux d'Architecture Moderne) meeting in Athens. In this sense, these borrowings were 'pure' – unencumbered by any real understanding of the original purpose of this or that feature of vernacular architecture. Building layouts and forms were transposed for their own sake, for their architectural qualities alone.

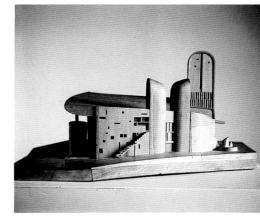

≈ Le Corbusier's beautiful model of the chapel at Ronchamp. It was built with wood in one purifying colour to emphasize the basic form of the structure. The use of unifying white to display such models to best effect arises from a lesson learned by observing the delineation of line and form in the Mediterranean villages.

Another Modernist architect who was directly and lastingly influenced by the white villages of Greece was Le Corbusier. In 1911, after working as a draughtsman in the Berlin office of Peter Behrens, Le Corbusier, along with his friend Auguste Klipstein, spent seven months travelling in the region. It is a journey which Le Corbusier regarded as hugely important to his development as a plastic artist. Indeed, he recorded the journey and had it published in 1965 as *Voyage d'Orient* (war having postponed original publication in 1914). The journey and the book must have been very special to Le Corbusier because he took it on himself to edit the text personally.

Architects tended not to copy individual features, such as window- and door-openings, since they were usually very simple and unremarkable. What proved more exportable was the overall character of the vernacular settlements as sculptural compositions. They were particularly attractive to designers of mass housing, since they appeared to provide useful models for combining a large number of nearly identical units into a form which held considerable promise as an attractive three-dimensional composition, while avoiding the conventional monolithic block or slab formats of public housing. Examples of what was later dubbed the urban megastructure can be found in the work of many pioneers of Modern architecture – J. J. P. Oud in Holland (Seaside Housing 1917) and Henry Sauvage in Paris (Flats, rue des Amiraux 1924), among others.

These 'ant-hill' prototypes were developed further in the work of Sir Leslie Martin and his associates in Britain (St Pancras study 1957, unbuilt; and the Bloomsbury Centre, London 1963, project architect Patrick Hodgkinson); Moshe

≈ Moshe Safdie's Habitat project in Montreal (LEFT) suggests vernacular dwellings built into a natural geological form. The individual units, seemingly randomly stacked, provide a contemporary urban megastructure reminiscent of the white hillside village settlements. The project avoids the monolithic look of so many blocks of modern public housing in today's larger cities. Sir Denys Lasdun's project of residential buildings at Christ's College, Cambridge (OPPOSITE) draws on the vernacular to create an impression of a hillside village.

Safdie's Habitat in Montreal (and his other housing projects in Israel); Atelier 5 in Basle, Switzerland; and numerous resort hotel projects such as the Amathus Beach Hotel in Limassol, Cyprus, by The Architects' Collaborative (TAC), Boston. In all these examples a 'stepped section' configuration is developed to provide terraces or large balconies to each hotel room or apartment, the space within the building section being used

for support functions such as public rooms and service areas. Whatever their architectural merits and power as sculptural objects, these stepped section buildings, which bear a strong and often intended relationship to vernacular hillside housing, have usually proved expensive and complex to construct. Several generations of architects have laboured to invent credible uses for the large internal volumes that are formed by stepping the building section. The alternative is to leave the undercut 'back' of the section exposed: in such instances it is often a 'bad neighbour' in an urban setting. A prime example of this phenomenon is the 1964 residential building for Christ's College, Cambridge, by Sir Denys Lasdun, which offers a magnificent cascade of undergraduate rooms to the college while presenting a blank concrete wall and car park undercroft to the city street.

More convincing, because less forced, are the terraced schemes which have been tailored to existing slopes and hence create no unusable volume to the rear. Aalto's factory housing at Kauttua (1938–1940) responds to natural contours with an ingenious building section, and there are many examples of successful housing or hotel schemes where concept and contours marry well.

The second, and equally persuasive theme to emerge in contemporary architecture as a legacy from the Mediterranean vernacular is that of cluster planning – the arrangement of buildings in the form of compact 'village' groupings, often centred on a pedestrian spine which links the housing to community facilities such as schools.

The cluster format has proved particularly relevant to the design of new settlements for the Middle East, where the concept finds credible precedents in the traditional tribal groupings of the bedouin and the *haret* of the medieval Islamic city. Faced with the challenge of designing new desert settlements or extensions to existing urban areas where there are few pointers available from the context, architects have sought out, with increasing encouragement from their clients in the public ministries of Saudi Arabia or the Gulf States, methods of breaking down the sheer numbers of dwellings and support facilities required – a typical new community project may number 1500 houses on a single site – while at the same time providing a framework for traditional lifestyles and values. These planning concepts owe a great deal to the Mediterranean vernacular. Parallels can be found not only at the level of architectural detail but also, more fundamentally, in the basic grouping of dwellings. In Middle Eastern projects, houses will typically be clustered in groups of 15–20 around a common courtyard with a single access point; vehicles are allowed into this court, but its character is that of a mews or semi-private enclave shared by residents. Where possible, vehicles are grouped at the edge of the cluster, as at the Support Staff

≈ The pattern of architectural influences between the Mediterranean and Middle Eastern regions has become circular. Islamic traditions (many originating in the Persian and Byzantine Empires), techniques and features, as evidenced in the narrow street (ABOVE) in Marrakesh, and the Moroccan window (OPPOSITE), significantly shaped the vernacular architecture of the Mediterranean. Now contemporary architects are drawing inspiration from the Mediterranean region for Middle Eastern projects.

Housing for the University of Petroleum and Minerals in Dharan, Saudi Arabia, by the Houston architects Caudill Rowlett Scott (CRS), one of the finest projects of its kind in the Middle East. Cluster planning allows the designer to bring the individual dwellings close together while maintaining the necessary privacy for each family. A compact pattern of houses and private courtyards is developed, close in spirit to the urban texture of traditional Islamic settlements while providing modern space standards. There are many distinguished examples of such contemporary/traditional housing in the Arab world, designs that appear to echo the morphology of Mediterranean settlements.

The cluster approach also makes excellent climatic sense, since the compact layout of dwellings and their careful orientation automatically creates mutual shading of most external walls and alleyways. With experience and ingenuity, it is possible to design housing clusters which provide excellent protection from the harsh desert environment and which are a welcome alternative to the thoughtless copying of inappropriate 'western' villa prototypes.

These echoes of the Mediterranean in Arabia cannot be a coincidence; designers based in or in transit to the Middle East will be familiar with vernacular settlements from stop-overs or vacations. These forms and patterns will be uppermost in their minds when designing new settlements, even if the building programmes are much larger in scale. It is clearly dangerous to draw any direct parallel between a typical new Saudi Arabian house of 250 square metres and a two-room Greek dwelling for the same size of family, yet the principle of defensive design responding to the requirements of privacy and climate control does appear identical in both contexts. A further area of common ground is the relationship of housing clusters to their setting. As with the Mediterranean examples, many of the new desert communities sit in remote landscapes, making their compactness even more compelling.

Most of the new community projects in Arabia consist of public sector housing and hence are the responsibility of a single ministry and probably of a single design team. Variety within the tyranny of numbers becomes a matter of design ingenuity rather than the product of natural, organic development over time by many individuals, as it would be in the Mediterranean. To temper their scale, 'artificial' variations in dwelling layout and appearance are often introduced, supplied by landscape designs which illustrate individual themed species for each *haret*. A further parallel lies in the status given to particular buildings, a hierarchy of emphasis which will ensure prominence for the local mosque above the surrounding housing, much as a belltower or fortress might rise above a Greek village. Status is often reinforced by a network of 'view corridors' – pedestrian routes which provide uninterrupted vistas leading to the local mosques. Applying these

≈ Many contemporary Middle Eastern projects have been heavily influenced by the vernacular tradition of the Mediterranean basin, without neglecting more direct influences from their own heritage. This decorative detail from the Medersa (LEFT) in Marrakesh looks both backwards to an earlier era, and forwards, via Alhambra and the grand ornate period of Islamic culture in Spain, to the integration of Moorish effects. BELOW: typical Mediterranean vernacular close-knit grouping patterns.

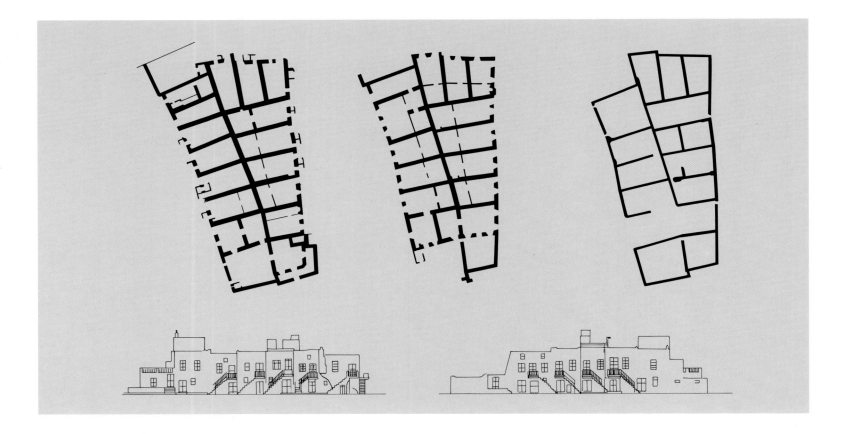

design devices, it is possible to make a large quantity of housing into a liveable and understandable structure.

Apart from their sybaritic virtues, these settlements have always held a particular appeal to pioneer Modernist architects such as Le Corbusier, whose early essays in Cubism found support in the ready-made 'Cubist' compositions of the Mediterranean. Although his interpretation of these settlements did not delve into their *raison d'être* or their sociology, still less into their functional structure, they did stimulate his architectonic intelligence in specific directions. They performed a cleansing, restorative function.

After locking swords with the French architectural establishment, Le Corbusier could draw strength from the undoubted plastic qualities of these village settlements. The simple act of whitewashing a dwelling stood for a whole realm of possibilities and virtues when transmuted by him into an operation of near-sacred significance. In Marc Besset's biography of the architect, he quotes Le Corbusier: 'Whitewash has been connected with the home of man since the birth of mankind; you burn stones, you pound them, you add water, you brush it on and the walls become the purest white, a white extraordinarily beautiful . . . whitewash is absolute; everything stands out from it or goes down on it absolutely, black on white, it is forthright and straightforward.'

Unlike other architects, who paid occasional lip-service to their summer memories of the Greek Islands, Le Corbusier retained his love of the vernacular virtues throughout his creative career. He continued to return to his *cabanon* at Cap Martin, a monastic cell less than four metres square and only a door high, which served him as a living and working space while he contemplated urban projects of world stature.

≈ The interior of Le Corbusier's chapel at Ronchamp resembles a vast cavern with its enveloping darkness and penetrating warm light. Through his study of Mediterranean architecture he would have been aware of the light qualities produced by built-over streets and narrow-apertured window-openings: Ronchamp is influenced both inside and out by the vernacular tradition.

Le Corbusier's love affair with the vernacular of the Mediterranean found direct expression in a clutch of related designs from the late 1940s that, unfortunately, were never built. These include the 'Roq' and 'Rob' complex at Cap Martin (terraced holiday homes clinging to the Mediterranean shore – 1949), and accommodation for the proposed pilgrimage centre at Sainte-Baume, above Toulon (1948). Both projects

≈ This ruined church in southern Italy (LEFT) exposes the workings of the barrel vaulting so common in the whitewashed villages. This simple technique is seen repeatedly throughout the works of such Modernist architects as Louis Kahn, Le Corbusier and Alvar Aalto, and provided them with a practical and adaptable architectural device. Combined with the basic building blocks of the vernacular – cubic form, indigenous materials, whitewash, and a few simple decorations, as seen in this scene (OPPOSITE) on Paros – barrel vaulting completed the stylistic repertoire of the Modernists who took inspiration from the Mediterranean tradition.

featured terraced apartment units roofed by concrete barrel vaults running lengthways which called up distinct echoes of vernacular roof forms. In the case of Sainte-Baume, the front facade was treated very much as an island dwelling on Santorini might have been, with a solid wall closing the end of the barrel vault above the main window-opening below. The result is a facade where mass dominates. At Cap Martin, by contrast, the front facade is fully glazed, with the barrel vault emerging as an arch bearing onto the cross wall. In both cases the seaward elevation is enlivened by the rhythm of the vaults riding above the housing and further enhanced by the staggering of units on plan. Unlike many subsequent imitations, these projects expose the underside of the barrel vault to the room below, with the play of sunlight and shadows as telling as it might be in a Greek vault a millennium old.

Although these projects were never constructed, we do have one example which is, in effect, a fragment of these larger designs – the summer house for Mme. de Mandrot near Toulon, with shallow parallel vaults of reinforced concrete. In this building natural materials predominate – exposed stone walls, timber and concrete surfaces. Le Corbusier's emphasis on the usage of natural materials certainly flowered in his later work, in which his 'white architecture' of the 1920s gave way to a full-blooded expression of texture and surface. Was this again a conscious gesture of homage to the vernacular? There is nothing unselfconscious or artisanal in Le Corbusier's use of these materials in his later buildings; they are all very knowingly assembled as sculptural compositions, much as French Cubist painter Georges Braque collected and joined together random fragments of 'found' materials. If this is noble savage rusticity, it is the cottage *orné* rather than the farmstead.

A more direct resonance is found in one of Le Corbusier's most powerful buildings, the pilgrimage chapel of Ronchamp, high in the foothills of the Vosges. Visitors to Ronchamp will find many aspects of the building which echo the Mediterranean vernacular – a whiteness unifying the massive external walls, tiny windows freely disposed in a wall several feet thick at its base (a thickness surely explained by sculptural rather than structural necessity), towers crowned by half domes that might be found on a Greek Island hillside, and everywhere the play of sunlight on the rough finishes. Within the chapel there are as many subtleties of light in all its forms as one might experience in the depths of some troglodytic chamber: light direct, light filtered through the primary colours of stained glass, light working inwards along the returns of the complex curving walls, light bouncing down from the oversailing roof plane. There is a wonderfully primeval, timeless quality within Ronchamp which we also associate with the Mediterranean vernacular. It is more than a superficial similarity of forms, and never a direct borrowing of vernacular elements. It is instead a celebration of the power of architecture as a plastic art, able to move and inspire by form alone.

≈ The pilgrimage chapel at Ronchamp (OPPOSITE, ABOVE AND RIGHT), is Le Corbusier's *tour de force*, and the most spectacularly successful structure to claim its heritage in the influence of the Mediterranean vernacular. It combines many, if not all, of the elements seen so commonly throughout this volume: massive external walls unified by white; tiny aperture window-openings; domes; a sloping roof; and a variety of interesting textures seen at their best in the full Mediterranean sun. The result transcends pastiche: it takes the finest of the vernacular and interprets the elements into a structure which has an integrity of its own.

Where Le Corbusier led, many of his distinguished disciples have followed. Josep Lluis Sert, one-time professor of architecture at Harvard and the designer of some of the most successful buildings of the Corbusian school, drew from his own Spanish ancestry with designs which play skilfully with solid, sculptural masses relieved by a pattern of elegant openings, or which develop the great potential of the patio in the planning of the Mediterranean house. Sert's sophisticated compositional technique and his ability to recreate the essence of a tradition without pastiche epitomize the strength and endurance of the vernacular.

A later generation of European architects has been inspired by the village vernacular. Far north in Finland, there is a school of architects which has adapted the Corbusian canon to powerful effect. Its members play complex games with the elements of 'white architecture' to produce compositions of great richness and subtlety. Their construction is closest in spirit to the white architecture of Le Corbusier and its Mediterranean antecedents in the new cultural centre for the lakeside town of Pieksämäki, by the leading young partnership of Gullichsen, Kairamo and Vormala.

A FUTURE FOR THE VERNACULAR

Writing in support of Bernard Rudofsky's New York exhibition *Architecture Without Architects*, the architect Pietro Belluschi defined the vernacular as 'a communal art, not produced by a few intelligences or specialists, but by the spontaneous and continuing activity of a whole people with a common heritage, acting under a community of experience.' In our time, this might seem to place the vernacular in the camp of what has been labelled 'community architecture', a phenomenon which was identified by the architectural professions in America and Britain (or at least by the Royal Institute of British Architects) in the mid–1980s. Variously dubbed as democratic, putting-people-first, responsive, down-to-earth, user-friendly, ecological, life-enhancing and even morally superior by those within the approved tribe of community architects, the movement, or more arguably, the bandwagon, appeared unstoppable. After all, what could be more acceptable than designers bending over backwards to involve their clients at every stage of their project?

At the time, certain veteran architects were obliged to remind the zealots of community architecture that their newfound approach to clients and to the task of forging an appropriate design solution to their client's needs was hardly original. 'Good' architects had been listening carefully to their clients ever since Ictinus got the Parthenon job. It was part of the architect's remit to interpret the needs, both functional

≈ Belluschi's claim that the vernacular is 'a communal art, not produced by a few intelligences or specialists' could not be better illustrated than in these scenes from Mykonos (ABOVE) and Essaouira, Morocco (OPPOSITE): their architectural success derives from the collective effort of the community.

≈ Perhaps the starting point for any investigation of the vernacular tradition, The Alhambra, Granada (LEFT) is one of the few remaining buildings in Spain constructed at the height of the Islamic occupation. Though not vernacular in any sense of the word, it exemplifies the Saracenic style which has influenced Mediterranean architecture at all levels for six hundred years. This group of images from Mykonos (OPPOSITE) again emphasizes one of the key lessons that today's architects can learn from the vernacular: that it is a community architecture, constructed by the community to meet the community's needs. It is not imposed on the community by an individual designer or a town planning department. These seemingly effortless but aesthetically delightful scenes are the product of hundreds of hands working in concert within an almost intuitively understood system.

and symbolic, of the client and to translate them into built form. In some cases the architect has been required to act as honest broker for a number of client groups, negotiating perhaps a common development brief for a complex inner-city site. If the results on the ground appear unconvincing and arrogant, the blame can more often be laid at the developer's door, or rest with the local authority who insisted that a mammoth shopping development go ahead 'to protect local jobs' and so on.

Such observations might appear to be unrelated to the Mediterranean village vernacular, but as pressure for development in these settlements increases they are more relevant than ever. If we take Pietro Belluschi's assertion again, that the vernacular is the product of communal rather than individual activity, then there appears to be no room for the trained specialist, the tutored, knowing and hence self-conscious designer: everything, every stroke of the whitewashing brush, every new window-opening or balcony will be guided by the collective instinct and good sense of the village community.

What then are the real lessons to be drawn by contemporary designers from the vernacular traditions of the Mediterranean

basin? There are certainly enough negative examples of unthinking recent projects that totally ignore the existing settlements which adjoin them, or elbow themselves clumsily into their midst, all in the name of 'progress'. While no serious designer would advocate a return to the copy–catting of vernacular features or urban forms (nothing could be more patronizing to the host community) there is the continuing temptation to transpose architectural elements wholesale into new structures to achieve a degree of instant credibility. How simple it is to select, say, barrel vaulting and use it to roof, willy-nilly, every holiday villa in the Mediterranean.

On the assumption that a large development is contemplated as an extension of, or in the vicinity of, the type of settlement celebrated in this volume, there are certain principles which should govern the layout and design. Firstly, apparent scale. Simple, prismatic masses can sometimes succeed – witness the clean prisms of some Mediterranean hotels – but these require an open sweep of rugged landscape as a setting to enhance their power as pristine artifacts counterpointing nature. If the new accommodation is to be integrated with the existing urban fabric, then its scale and bulk must be broken down to the scale of the existing townscape, which for all its unity of colour, materials and grain can still be read as a group of individual dwellings.

Just how much new development is acceptable in a particular context? This quantum can only be determined after thorough study of the settlement, of its skylines, roofscape, street pattern, key buildings and sites where appropriate development would reinforce the existing form. In some instances, the settlement can only accept a very limited quantity of additional building; the correct solution, if this amount is still to be included, may be a mix of conversion and rebuilding, retaining some of the existing building envelopes. It goes without saying that the present prevailing materials, skylines and scale should serve as the starting point for the designer.

≈ Integration of new buildings with old is made simple by tradition. In well-maintained vernacular settlements such as Mykonos (ABOVE) where scale and materials are carefully matched, development goes almost unnoticed, and the unifying whitewash soon melds neighbouring buildings of differing ages seamlessly together. There is room also for personal statement, as in this window (OPPOSITE): where it is in keeping with the style – here traditional patterns and colours are employed – it can be assimilated without detracting from the effect of the whole.

In this respect, some of the best examples of successful integration of new buildings into existing urban fabric can be found in the islands off the Dalmatian coast, where Yugoslavian architects have proved skilful in a conservation approach to redundant village buildings with a careful insertion of new buildings which avoids pastiche. Similarly, in the towns of North Italy master architect Carlo Scarpa has provided a successful integration of contemporary and vernacular designs in such buildings as the Banca Popolare in Verona. At its best this intervention passes almost unnoticed; the settlement gains from controlled tourism and the future of important historic buildings is assured.

These concepts confirm that it is possible to design new accommodation that is sympathetic to the vernacular. Aside from the problem of the mass hotel, which is probably best handled as a freestanding element distanced from the existing settlement, there are vernacular themes which translate very successfully into new buildings – white solids punctuated with deep-set openings; a delight in 'thickness' and contour of wall returns; window-openings that respect traditional vertical proportions; concentrated areas of detail and colour against a predominant white background, and the use of natural materials for functional elements such as balconies and external screens. The deft combination of these elements should ensure that the resultant building emerges as a good neighbour and takes its place in the existing townscape. But it will only do so if the other 'rules' of vernacular composition are followed – attention to sky and roof lines; fragmentation of the building mass into house-scaled units; setting new facades on the existing building line; basing the development pattern on open patios or squares, and retaining existing street lines or site profiles.

While the design principles for successful intervention in a Mediterranean vernacular settlement can to some extent be codified, in reality there are powerful development pressures

≈ These villages are not theme parks or museums, but living communities. Fortunately they are in the stewardship of those most likely to preserve their integrity: their inhabitants. The populace of such settlements as Mykonos (BELOW) and Sperlonga (RIGHT) have been aware for many years of the potential threats that their beauty engenders, and long ago took steps to ensure that their architectural heritage would be protected.

which mitigate against architectural quality. It is so much simpler, it seems, to put up a single concrete box and dress it with 'vernacular' features than to mature a design which sits well in its context and is, in the best sense of the word, timeless.

So, what does the future hold for the whitewashed villages of the Mediterranean? They are working communities, not museums or theme parks and are subject to the usual village cycles of falling employment, ageing and depopulation. While it would be perverse to preserve them in their present state under a well-intentioned but sterile custodianship – to encapsulate them, as it were, in a frozen fairy tale world – there is no doubt that many of them are vulnerable to the pressures of incoming development. It only takes a few ill-conceived projects to undermine or destroy the precious visual unity of these village settlements. A visitor to the Spanish coast will appreciate just how much damage can so easily be caused by unthinking design, even if justified as a necessary consequence of economic development. These communities are even more vulnerable as a result of their relative isolation; progress comes in large, seductive lumps of cash even if acceptance brings far less attractive lumps of concrete in its wake.

Just what then is the message of the Mediterranean vernacular, the white villages, for the architect in the 1990s? Perhaps the lessons should, rather, be addressed to society at large, since one of the undoubted delights of these settlements is the quality of what has come to be known as the 'public realm' – all those streets, squares, spaces and odd corners beyond the houses which form the village, town or city. Amidst the public squalour of our cities the example of husbandry and pride given by these Mediterranean villages shines out. A direct comparison of the two cases is perhaps unfair, since the scale and complexity of our cities is far removed from the village cosmos, but we would be hard put to replicate the latter's standards of public housekeeping and local pride. Nor can we

claim that the villages appear as delightful, inspiring and strong because of some unseen set of design rules imposed upon an unwilling population. A whitewashed oil-can full of geraniums does not appear on a village porch by edict or decree; thresholds are not scrubbed according to any master schedule; no T-square traced that street line. It is through this freedom for the individual to build himself a home within the fabric of the village, without damaging it, that these communities can offer us a modest but essential signpost.

≈ 189

Bibliography

AALTO, ALVAR

Works
Alec Tiranti; London; 1963

ATROSHENKO, V.I., JUDITH COLLINS

The Origins of the Romanesque: Near Eastern Influences on European Art
Lund Humphries;
London; 1985

BANHAM, REYNER

Theory and Design in the First Machine Age
The Architectural Press;
London; 1960

BANHAM, REYNER

Age of the Masters: A personal view of modern architecture
The Architectural Press;
London; 1975

BLAKE, PETER

The Master Builders
W. W. Norton;
New York; 1976

CARVER, NORMAN F. JR

Iberian Villages
Documan Press; Kalamazoo,
Michigan; 1985

CARVER, NORMAN F. JR

Italian Hill Towns
Documan Press; Kalamazoo,
Michigan; 1985

LE CORBUSIER

Ouevre Complete
W. Boesinger/Editions
Girsberger; Zurich; 1955

LE CORBUSIER

Towards a New Architecture
The Architectural Press;
London; 1927

CRESWELL, K.A.C

A Short Account of Early Muslim Architecture
Penguin Books; London; 1958

DE WOLFE, IVOR

The Italian Townscape
The Architectural Press;
London; 1967

DICKS, BRIAN

The Greek Islands
Robert Hale; London; 1988

DURRELL, LAWRENCE

The Greek Islands
Faber & Faber;
London; 1978

FLEIG, KARL

Alvar Aalto; Works and Projects
Architecktur Artemis;
Zurich; 1974

JENCKS, CHARLES

Le Corbusier and the Tragic View of Architecture
Penguin Books; London; 1987

LASDUN, DENYS

A Language and a Theme
RIBA Publications;
London; 1976

MAHOLY-NAGY, SIBYL

Native Genius in Anonymous Architecture
Horizon Press;
New York; 1957

ED. PHILIPPIDES, DR. DIMITRI

Greek Traditional Architecture
Melissa; Athens; 1983

RAPPAPORT, AMOS

House Form and Culture
Prentice Hall Inc;
New York; 1969

RASMUSSEN, STEEN EILER

Experiencing Architecture
Chapman & Hall;
London; 1959

RUDOFSKY, BERNARD

Architecture Without Architects
Museum of Modern Art;
New York; 1964
(Reprint: University of
New Mexico Press; 1988)

≈ Mykonos

INDEX

ACKNOWLEDGEMENTS

All pictures not specifically credited here are by the author, V. I. Atroshenko. Further material was provided by the following:

Mr. Robert O'Dea: 138: 147: 148 (left): 149 (left and right): 167: 174: 175: 176: 179: 183: 185 (all four pictures): 187: 190

Arcaid: 141 (top, Tim Soar: bottom right, Richard Bryant)

The Architectural Association: 143 (top left, Kosta Mathey): 144 (background texture, Kosta Mathey): 152 (above left, Bernard Fielden): 153 (top right, Geoff Smythe): 155 (bottom right, Thalis Argyropaulis): 158 (Ewing Gallaway): 159 (top left, Andrew Minchin: top right, Hillenbrand): 162 (Andrew Minchin): 165 (top right, Miss Mary Parsons): 168 (Michael Kim): 171 (James Gowan): 172 (Rita de Pierro): 173 (Peter Look): 177 (Peter Bond): 178 (Thalis Argyropaulis): 180 (Danielle Tinero): 181 (top, Peter Bond: bottom, D. Plummer)

Edifice: 143 (bottom, Edifice/Darley): 150 (Edifice/Lewis): 151 (above left, Edifice/Lewis: bottom, Edifice/Darley): 153 (bottom, Edifice/Darley): 155 (top left, Edifice/Darley: right, Edifice/Darley): 156 (top, Edifice/Darley): 156 (Edifice/Darley): 160 (Edifice/Darley): 163 (Edifice/Darley): 184 (Edifice/Darley)

The publishers offer grateful thanks to all these sources.